Unworkable Conservatism:
Small Government, Freemarkets, and Impracticality

UNWORKABLE CONSERVATISM

SMALL GOVERNMENT, FREEMARKETS, AND IMPRACTICALITY

MAX J. SKIDMORE

Westphalia Press
An Imprint of the Policy Studies Organization
Washington, DC
2017

Unworkable Conservatism:
Small Government, Freemarkets, and Impracticality

All Rights Reserved © 2017 by Policy Studies Organization

Westphalia Press
An imprint of Policy Studies Organization
1527 New Hampshire Ave., NW
Washington, D.C. 20036
info@ipsonet.org

ISBN-10: 978-1-63391-616-6
ISBN-13: 1-63391-616-2

Cover and interior design by Jeffrey Barnes
jbarnesbook.design

Daniel Gutierrez-Sandoval, Executive Director
PSO and Westphalia Press

Updated material and comments on this edition
can be found at the Westphalia Press website:
www.westphaliapress.org

The principles accepted by modern American "conservatives" and libertarians emerged in the 18th century, crafted carefully to protect the people from the powerful. As they have evolved, or devolved, over the last half century or so, they now are carefully crafted to protect the powerful from the people.

CONTENTS

CHAPTER 1
Introduction: Looking at Things as They Are
1

CHAPTER 2
"Conservative" Ideological Principles
and Social Programs
17

CHAPTER 3
Shining Light on Dark Politics:
An Essay and Review
37

CHAPTER 4
Policy Insights from Party History
101

CHAPTER 5
Could the National Popular Vote Interstate
Compact Save Us from the Electoral College?
An Analysis and a Word of Caution
147

CHAPTER 1
INTRODUCTION: LOOKING AT THINGS AS THEY ARE

The principles accepted by modern American "conservatives" and libertarians emerged in the eighteenth century, crafted carefully to protect the people from the powerful. As they have evolved, or devolved, over the last half century or so, they now are carefully crafted to protect the powerful from the people.

Learn to See, Not Just Look—

This book looks at things that should be obvious, but obviously are not. It often is difficult to recognize reality when it contradicts years of accepting something as true, when it is false. The late Will Rogers once remarked something to the effect that, "it ain't what people don't know that's so dangerous—it's what people *know* that *just ain't so!*" Many of the ideas that large numbers of Americans accept as true in history and politics simply are not correct, and as often as not the reason for their mistaken beliefs is that they have been deliberately encouraged to accept false ideas, because powerful interests—the late Aldous Huxley referred to them as "Mind Manipulators"[1]—benefit from their misunderstandings.

Some beliefs remain widespread when they are so easily disproven as to be almost laughable. Here are some prominent examples: "America's health care system is the best in the world." "Poor people in American live better than ordinary citizens in other countries." "Government is always inefficient." "Private industry and programs always operate more efficiently than government." "Regulation always gets in the way of business." "Crime and violence go down when all decent citizens carry firearms." "Minimum wage laws reduce jobs." "The economy always is more robust when taxes are low and regulations are minimal or nonexistent." "Universal health programs reduce choice and lower the quality of

1

care." "Business would take good care of workers if there were no restrictive government regulations." "When businesses receive tax cuts, they raise workers' salaries." "When Canadians get sick, they stream south to the United States to get good health care."

This last one is especially silly. If it were true, Canadians would have to be far more wealthy than Americans. America's healthcare is the world's most expensive, by a long shot; so expensive, in fact, that almost no one can afford it without excellent health insurance. Canadians would have to pay for US care out of pocket—*since they do not have health insurance policies!*

Americans by now should join the rest of the world and recognize the danger of widespread availability of firearms. Citing homicide figures is inadequate. Guns play a huge role in suicides, and the horrendous spectacle of mass killings has become an American phenomenon. Just the weekend before this was written, three citizens were gunned down on the street in Lawrence, Kansas—a pleasant university town in the Midwest, and the home of the University of Kansas. That tragedy, extreme as it was, failed even to make headlines outside of the local area. That was not only because such things have become almost routine in the United States, but also because a maniac in Las Vegas at roughly the same time committed the largest mass shooting in American history, wounding hundreds, and killing roughly 60 people at random. So much for the effect of the "guns for all" mentality.

Of course, the White House commented that it would be "premature" to discuss gun control. Right wing broadcaster Sean Hannity went further, raging that calling for gun control after the Las Vegas tragedy was "shameful." Note that what Hannity considered "shameful" was less the killings than any discussion about how to end them. One fact stands out clearly: if no gun is available to someone planning a crime or suicide, that person will not have a gun to use. Guns, however, are widely available in the United States to virtually anyone.

Another fact should stand out just as clearly. It was not until *District of Columbia* v. *Heller*, in 2008, that the Court declared an individual right to own and carry a firearm. That decision was the result of a judiciary packed with conservatives from the Federalist Society, and a long campaign by the National Rifle Association to re-interpret the Second Amendment. No less a conservative icon than former Chief Justice Warren Burger (a conservative Republican Nixon appointee) said on PBS in 1990 that the notion of an individual right to own and carry was "a fraud on the American public."[2]

A quarter century later, it was the late Associate Justice Antonin Scalia, who wrote the decision completely revising and infusing a new meaning to the Second Amendment. The noted "originalist" found an original understanding of the Second Amendment that decades of interpretations from scholars and judges had never found there. As one writer said of Scalia:

> Much of his jurisprudence protected the powerful, such as corporations with money to spend on elections, and white plaintiffs against affirmative action. And when he gave the Constitution a meaning taken from recent politics, such as the echoes between his Second Amendment jurisprudence and the National Rifle Association's propaganda, his method concealed it. His originalism promised to hold the Constitution above politics, but his judicial opinions reinforced the impression that his judging was only politics by other means.[3]

Addressing Misconceptions (However Fundamental) That Are Especially Dangerous—

It requires very little scrutiny of comments relating to the elections of 2016 to discover an opinion that appeared to be fairly widespread, especially among those on either extreme of right and left. However irrational it was, it encouraged enormous disruption, and to many people had a romantic appeal that very likely influenced the elections: "When conditions are not to our liking, we need to 'shake things up,' to cause chaos. Then all will improve."

They will not. What chaos causes is more chaos. Ultimately, as history demonstrates, it brings severe repression.

This book will not seek to correct all misconceptions, but it will demonstrate that some very widespread, and very influential, beliefs among Americans are wrong. Modern Republicans and Democrats tend to believe very different things. That's politics. Difference of opinion is what creates parties in the first place. Politics is not like science. A proposition in science may be accepted or rejected based upon the results of empirical research. Politics, on the other hand, deals with values, and values are not susceptible to scientific standards of proof. All well and good. What too often is overlooked, though, is that values should not be accepted—or considered as acceptable—if they rest on assumptions that clearly are false.

It might seem to be heresy to question the fundamental assumptions that many Americans maintain. It is not heresy, though, if those beliefs are false. It especially is not heresy if those false beliefs are destructive.

The most fundamental principles that modern American conservatives profess, are first, that minimal government, especially at the national level, provides the greatest efficiency, the best service to the people, and the greatest degree of personal liberty. Be sure to note, however, that conservatives speak in terms of personal liberty, what they usually mean is something far different: the "freedom" to accumulate, and to spend funds, without limit. Second, conservatives argue that the best way to maintain personal freedom and prosperity for all is to keep taxes very low. Third, conservatives consider the existence of any but the most minimal governmental regulation violates liberty, destroys efficiency, and is inconsistent with prosperity and property rights.

Considering how widespread these beliefs are among Americans, it is easier than it might seem to demonstrate that they are wrong. First, what they propose tends to be very difficult to implement. Second, if implemented, the results are almost guaranteed to be unsatisfactory. The nature of conservative principles is such that they encourage huge concentrations of power, economic and otherwise, in private hands with no method to keep them in check. They thus foster authoritarian practices, and add greater protections for those who hold power—this has been deliberate; some of those who provided the philosophical rationale for these practices were in fact candid about their intentions (see Chapter 4). Moreover, they encourage conservatives to flout any general understandings of appropriate conduct when they consider it necessary to achieve or to hold power. This leads them to become ever more extreme in their behavior, and encourages violence and disrespect for society's fundamental institutions. The elevation of Donald Trump to the presidency is merely a culmination of decades of increasingly cavalier conduct from conservatives as they throw aside any understood limits on political conduct.

One example from the discussion above, the revised understanding greatly limiting—although not completely eliminating—the right of governments to restrict firearms is an example of a "conservative" policy that ultimately was implemented. It provided protection for firearms manufacturers that shielded them and gun dealers from lawsuits. The effect of that policy verifies the observation that, when conservative policies actually to make it into law, the result is unsatisfactory. In this case, it has been completely disastrous, in having achieved for the United States, the unenviable status of becoming the world leader in the frequency of mass murder by firearm.

An equally good example of the principle that small-government policies are not feasible is the obsession of Republicans with President Obama's Affordable Care Act. They opposed it; fair enough. They refused to cooperate with the Obama administration to make it more to their liking; fair enough. They voted against it; fair enough.

After it passed, however, they defamed it in every way possible. They charged that Democrats passed it in secrecy, and that "no one had read the bill." They lied.

The process was as open as any legislative process in history. Everything was available online for 18 months or so of consideration. Both House and Senate committees processed the proposals and held public hearings. There were five separate committees in all. The Democrats tried constantly to obtain Republican support, and made countless revisions to accommodate Republican wishes, but Republicans all maintained party discipline, and no Republican supported the Act.

What should be recognized is that *any* complicated program implementing legislation requires legislative changes, improvements, through the years for the greatest efficiency. These are necessary to adapt such programs to unforeseen conditions. With "Obamacare," though, this did not happen. Republicans blocked every effort to improve the Affordable Care Act.

Also, they continually attempted to repeal the program. That was unusual, but remained within the normal realm of American politics. What was out of the ordinary, and what violated all norms of civic consciousness, and conscience, was that they continually, and openly, worked to make the Act fail. They did everything possible to ensure that it would not be successful. Despite all their efforts, and despite their rhetoric, "Obamacare" has generally been very successful.

In the 2016 elections, Mr. Trump, and all Republicans elected to the majority in the House and the majority in the Senate, declared their intention to "repeal Obamacare." Sometimes, to make it more palatable, they said, "to repeal and replace." Despite complete control of all levers of government, despite numerous efforts, and despite unanimous commitment to repeal, to Mr. Trump's great outrage, they could not do so. They vowed to continue efforts to repeal, and they are doing so. It is possible that sometime they might succeed.

Nevertheless, their experience to date makes plain just how difficult it is to implement the Republican commitment to minimal government. The reason is that the potential for great damage to the people is so great. Again—and this should be repeated until it penetrates the propaganda-induced barriers to clear thought—everyone should understand that the less power the government has, the fewer resources there are to protect citizens against predatory corporations and other sources of private power.

Effective government is all the people have to shield them against hostile private forces; and yes, the people themselves need to keep careful watch on government, but they do have the power to check it when required. If the Republicans had succeeded in repealing the ACA, an enormous segment of the population would suddenly have lost its health protection. Despite this background, Trump and congressional Republicans continue both openly and covertly to sabotage their nemesis, the hated "Obamacare" (hated primarily because it was President Obama who signed it into law). They hope thereby to cause so much trouble in the program that the people will react against it. It violates all norms of acceptable political practice when a political party cynically works to destroy an existing program by doing everything they can to ensure that it performs poorly.

Conservatives have employed all sorts of tactics to shape political reality in their favor. A major example is their encouragement of the Tea Party (originally, some of its members said the name stood for Taxed Enough Already, despite the low levels of taxes that prevail in the United States—far lower than a few decades ago). Oddly, despite their reputation, studies of Tea Party members demonstrate that they really do not oppose government programs. They tend to love Social Security, Medicare, and programs that benefit them directly. What they resent bitterly is any sort of government benefits going to others whom they believe are not worthy. Hence, the Internet lies that charge that any "illegal immigrant" immediately upon arrival becomes eligible for Social Security, full healthcare, and on and on—all of which is completely false—but which feeds their anger.

The resentment of "my tax dollars" going to support someone else is similar to the tactics employed by wealthy power holders in the south in the late nineteenth and early twentieth centuries. Startled by efforts to develop cooperative resistance among blacks and poor whites—who had much the same economic difficulties and the same interests—the power holders cynically fanned the flames of racial prejudice to cause resentment among the poor whites against their black brothers and sisters.

The result was that racial hatred overruled (one might say trumped) economic concerns by blinding the poor whites to their true interests. In modern America, the constant refrain of "the taxpayers' money" helps to accomplish the same purpose.

Few people, including most members of Congress, understand that this cliché is not really accurate. The belief is that every dollar the government spends must come from somewhere, such as taxation, or borrowing. There is little recognition that the U.S. government (not state or local governments) continually creates money.

As counter-intuitive as it sounds, there is no direct correlation between the national government's spending and the amount of tax money that it takes in. Anyone who resents benefits going to another person should recognize that cancelling all such benefits would not lower his or her taxes, nor would greatly increasing the benefits automatically cause those taxes to increase. Recognizing that, of course, would not necessarily cause resentments to cease, given human nature. It seems easier to generate resentments, sadly, than to eliminate them. One of the tactics that conservatives openly, and gleefully, employ is to encourage a perpetual rage. Their allies, talk radio and the Fox News Network, are their foot soldiers in these efforts. Many such conservatives find great sport in insulting and attempting to cause discomfort among "liberals," or, as they often put it, "libtards."

This, of course, would have been impossible before the Reagan presidency because of the long-standing and very successful Fairness Doctrine that mandated, not equal time, but that some effort be made on the public's airwaves, radio and television, to ensure that all major points of view have some representation. President Reagan's Federal Communications Commission, asserting that mandating fairness gave an advantage to "liberals," eliminated the doctrine. This brings to mind Stephen Colbert's quip in his previous incarnation that "reality has a well-known liberal bias." At any rate, Congress thereupon passed legislation reinstating it. President Reagan, also not wanting to give unfair advantage to liberals by mandating fairness, vetoed the act, killing the doctrine.

Blaming victims, similarly, has a long history. Perhaps the most cogent recent example is Mr. Trump's condemnation of Puerto Ricans for having been struck by a hurricane, and of course for not praising him adequately.

To examine more closely the assertion that conservative principles are not feasible, consider that in modern times, no extreme conservative has ever been elected to the presidency who did not then disappoint his supporters. Always, their complaint (ignoring the "law of holes," that to get out of one, it is necessary to stop digging) is that the president was not conservative enough.

Since the Civil War, America's major parties tended to be pragmatic, not highly ideological. This has changed, dramatically. Lest anyone underestimate the extent to which the Republican Party in recent decades has departed from the historical standards of America's major parties, note the ideological extremism of the Republican candidates in 2012 and 2016. All who sought the nomination claimed to be "more like Ronald Reagan," than the others, and all professed to be "more conservative" than any other (one bragged that he had been a "severely conservative" governor). That had little to do with policy, and everything to do with ideological fervor—or tribal identity. Oddly, the exception seemed to be Mr. Trump. He was not an ideological conservative, but he appealed to all the conservatives' basic prejudices even more than those who were ideologically conservative; perhaps he succeeded because was far less restrained in his comments.

Since before the election of Ronald Reagan in 1980, the right wing of the Republican Party has attempted to elect presidents devoted to what passes these days for "conservatism." The most dramatic instance was the ill-fated candidacy of Barry Goldwater ("Extremism in the defense of liberty is no vice! And let me remind you also that moderation in the pursuit of justice is no virtue"). It was Goldwater whom Lyndon Johnson trounced in the election of 1964. In a historical sense, America's modern conservatives adhere to an ideology that to a large extent is closer to classical, laissez-faire liberalism, than to "conservatism" elsewhere.

As noted, today's American conservatism involves small and limited government, especially at the national level, few or no regulations affecting business, keeping taxes as low as possible, and paring services (other than police and military) down to a minimum. As also noted, the essays that comprise the chapters that follow demonstrate that these principles are very difficult to implement, and, if ever implemented, are unsatisfactory even to their supporters.

As for the balanced budgets that were so important to Republicans until after Reagan's election, they lost their emotional appeal. About the time Reagan took office, the party began to elevate tax cuts above any consideration of balanced budgets, or even above any notion of keeping deficits at the lowest levels feasible. As a matter of practicality, the more they insist on reducing taxes—in spite of their supply-side fairy tales—the less they can permit themselves to be concerned about the resulting increase in deficits.

This reflected the influence of enormously wealthy contributors. Their primary political aim had become the elimination of every possible regulation that affected their businesses, and the reduction as far as possible of any tax they must pay. They had convinced themselves that their motivations were noble. Far from being greedy and self-centered, they were committed to principle; as patriotic Americans, they were devoted to "freedom." Their definition of freedom, of course, was limited. To them, freedom was the ability to accumulate without limit, and to do what they wished with their fortunes without interference.

Goldwater's defeat had been so huge that commentators pondered at the time whether the Republican Party could survive. Four years later, it not only bounced back, it elected Richard Nixon as president. Nixon played both sides. He was receptive to some social programs, and even advocated a guaranteed annual income, in the form of a negative income tax that would help lift people from poverty. At the same time, in the form of "nudge nudge, wink, wink," he catered to southern racial animosities, and embarked upon his "southern strategy" to attract southern racists into the Republican Party. This was hardly difficult, since LBJ's Civil Rights Act of 1964 and Voting Rights Act of 1965 were the sources of widespread outrage throughout the white south, and already had pushed southern racists out of the Democratic Party.

Nixon's own lust for power, his determination to "screw my enemies," as he put it, and willingness to disregard ethics and reasonable restraints that had become "the rules of the game," led to his being forced from office. His successor, Gerald Ford, served a truncated term, and lost to former Georgia Governor Jimmy Carter.

Carter, in turn, after one term, lost to former actor and former Governor of California, Ronald Reagan. Reagan had been the darling of right-wing extremists, and until he secured the Republican nomination, had represented the far-right fringe of the party. With the imprimatur of a major party's approval, much of what had been extremism on the right, moved into mainstream respectability. Ultra conservatives were delighted. Despite his saintly status among today's Republicans, however, Reagan proved disappointing; he had an unexpected interest in governing well, and to be more practical than his alarming rhetoric had led them to believe.

Avoiding criticism of Reagan personally, their cries of "Let Reagan be Reagan" increased as his 8 years in office progressed. He had cut taxes drastically, but had been so alarmed at the result that he raised them numerous times. Although he continued, and intensified, Nixon's southern strategy, he also freely worked with the hated Democrats. Initially, he tried attacked Social Security, but when the opposition his attacks generated was so great, he promised not to do it again. He remained true to his promise. He was the last president to sign an amnesty for undocumented immigrants. Today's Republicans by and large have forgotten this, or those too young to remember may never had heard about the cracks in the armor of Reagan's ideological fervor.

Despite his current mythological status, Reagan had found that ideological conservatism would not work, recognized reality, and adjusted. Vice President George H. W. Bush, succeeded Reagan (the first time a sitting vice president had been elected president since Martin Van Buren in 1836), and he, too, recognized reality. He found that his boast of "read my lips, no new taxes" was impractical. Casting ideology aside in favor of sound government, he did the unthinkable: he signed into law a tax increase. His conservative supporters turned against him.

Republicans were aghast when Bill Clinton, a Democrat, became president. As with Barack Obama, although obviously without the racism, Republicans fought Clinton vigorously. In an especially vengeful mood, even when it was obvious that they could not achieve the necessary two thirds of the Senate for conviction, they impeached him. They failed even to reach a majority of the Senate when several Republicans joined the Democrats for acquittal. Clinton's popularity soared.

Replacing Clinton after his two terms in office was former President George H. W. Bush's son, George W. The younger Bush campaigned as a moderate, calling for "compassionate conservatism." In office, though, in close cooperation with his hard line vice president Richard Cheney, he functioned as a movement conservative (the term that emerged to describe the most fervent, conservative ideologues). He succeeded, skillfully but briefly, in uniting the country after the attacks of 9/11, and pushed the movement conservatives' agenda of tax cuts, even while taking the country to war—probably the first such instance in the history of the world. He pushed for "faith-based" programs, sanctioned torture of prisoners, and won re-election in 2004. Feeling secure, he then moved to attack Social Security, and like Reagan, found the public reaction too strong. It was during his second term that economic disaster struck. In 2008, the economy collapsed, and the country plunged into the worst financial crisis since the Great Depression. He was forced to take some measures to help stem the economic downturn, and on October 3, 2008, he signed TARP (the Troubled Assets Relief Program, to purchase "toxic" assets). His conservative supporters reacted with horror.

Thus, despite his efforts to implement much of the movement conservative agenda, he lost favor with the ideologues. They thought he had become an advocate of "big government,"—he had become a "statist"—thus demonstrating, again, that the far right is not satisfied with whatever policies "conservative" presidents implement, or seek to implement.

Employing an Insightful Approach in Studying Conservatism—

One of the most insightful ways to deal with broad principles in modern writing has emerged in the form of the review, or review essay; that is, a review of a major work, or an essay that reviews several major works on the topic under consideration, and extends the analysis far enough beyond the reviewed work or works themselves as to constitute a creative work in its own right. One scholar even produced a book on the subject, arguing that under proper circumstances, the "review" has evolved to become a new literary form, taking its place beside such other creative literary forms as novels, short stories, poems, and the like.[4]

Along those lines, this examination of American conservatism uses the form of the creative review essay. There have been many useful works on conservatism in general, and American conservatism in particular. This has been especially true since the "godfather of American conservative presidents," Ronald Reagan, took office in 1981. This wealth of literature provides a core of material that renders American conservatism especially susceptible to thoughtful treatment by way of a review essay. This book incorporates three of those studies based on material that I have published previously.

This approach results in several findings that should be useful to those who make policy, if they will approach their tasks with open minds. Admittedly, open minds by definition are hardly to be found among ideologues, but it is important regardless to present them with accurate information.

Finally, in order to help in the efforts to discover some way to improve the current situation, the book examines that strange American phenomenon the electoral college. It discusses the difficulties that any attempt to change the system would involve, and examines a suggested approach that could possibly shift the system's emphasis away from electoral votes to the national popular vote, without the formidable obstacle of a constitutional amendment. That is the proposal for the National Popular Vote Interstate Compact. The analysis here suggests that the proposal could work. In fact, it is feasible, with one major caution. As it stands, it would rely upon the good faith of all parties to the process—an assumption that American political leaders will act honorably, and fulfill their agreements, even when that would lead to the election of their opponent.

Given the recent history of the Republican leadership, a history fully demonstrated in the following pages, it would not be safe to operate on such assurances without solid and irrevocable mechanisms that would ensure adherence to their promises by all parties.

Summing Up This Book's Approach, and Previewing Its Findings—

First, in common with many other works, this book presents conservatism in America as something different in many respects from conservatism elsewhere. To a large extent, what passes for conservatism in the United States, especially in recent years, is more closely akin to a variety of liberalism than to classic conservatism. There is nothing new in this observation (even the late Friedrich Hayek, an icon to the fiercest American conservatives, protested that he was not a conservative at all, but in fact was a liberal). It is necessary to repeat it, though, because it no doubt comes as a surprise to a general reader, and also because it places American conservatism in perspective, so that it can be studied realistically.

Second, this book demonstrates that the typical ideology of "small-government conservatism" in America under modern conditions is not a feasible approach to government. It is doomed to failure for several reasons. Its highly ideological nature is not buttressed by empirical findings, and is overly rigid. In many respects, it is more theological than political; more tribal than philosophical (hence, the damning nature of the powerful epithet among modern Republicans: "RINO"—Republican in Name Only).

Third, conservatism's ideological rigidity makes it extremely difficult, and in many instances completely impossible, to implement when in the form of important policy. Only in the most unusual of circumstances do its adherents manage to pass legislation incorporating conservatism's key points.

Fourth, in the rare instances when conservatives do manage to implement their programs, the results are unsuited to modern conditions. Thus, the results are unsatisfactory to all, even to conservatism's most fervent supporters. As indicated, people today fail to remember that during the presidency of the sainted Ronald Reagan, "Let Reagan be Reagan!" was the persistent cry of his disappointed supporters.

Finally, this book considers the well-meaning effort to improve the functioning of the electoral college, and gain the agreement of states to submit their electoral votes for the candidate who received the majority nationally of the popular vote. This "National Popular Vote Interstate Compact" is promising, but if implemented it will be founded upon a fatal flaw unless there are clear and powerful safeguards built in. That flaw is the requirement that political actors conduct themselves in good faith; that they will keep their word. As this book makes clear, it would be naïve to accept their assurances, based upon the examples of their conduct over the past few decades.

Notes

1   See my discussion of Huxley in Max J. Skidmore, "Populism and Its Perils: Language and Politics," *Annales Politologia* 22 (1) (2015).

2   Scholarship on this issue is extensive; for reporting see, e.g., Michael Waldman, "How the NRA Rewrote the Second Amendment," *Politico* (19 May 2014) http://www.politico.com/magazine/story/2014/05/nra-guns-second-amendment-106856.

3   Jedediah Purdy, "Scalia's Contradictory Originalism," *The New Yorker*, February 16, 2016, https://www.newyorker.com/news/news-desk/scalias-contradictory-originalism.

4   Joey Skidmore, *The Review as Art and Communication* (Newcastle Upon Tyne: Cambridge Scholars Publishing, 2013).

CHAPTER 2
"CONSERVATIVE" IDEOLOGICAL PRINCIPLES AND SOCIAL PROGRAMS[1]

Albert O. Hirschman, *The Rhetoric of Reaction: Perversity, Futility, Jeopardy*, Cambridge: The Belknap Press of Harvard University Press, 1991.

Thomas E. Mann and Norman J. Ornstein, *It's Even Worse Than It Looks/Was*, New and Expanded Edition, New York: Basic Books, 2016 [2012].

Frank S. Meyer, ed., *What Is Conservatism: A Timely, Important, and Provocative Examination of American Conservatism by Twelve Leading Conservative Thinkers and Spokesmen*, New York: Holt, Rinehart, and Winston, 1965.

Corey Robin, *The Reactionary Mind: Conservatism from Edmund Burke to Sarah Palin*, New York: Oxford University Press, 2011.

A Look at "Conservatism" in America—

In America, the second half of the twentieth century saw a burst of thought and activity under the banner of "conservatism," particularly after the presidency of Ronald Reagan. To be sure, what passes for conservatism in the United States often has a form more in common with classical liberalism than with true conservatism. This is especially the case with its more recent libertarian, anti-governmental, orientation. Note, for example, the arch-"conservative" icon of the American right, Austrian economist Friedrich A. von Hayek, the author in the mid-twentieth century of *The Road to Serfdom*,[2] the publisher of which burnished its conservative credentials with an abridged version widely distributed by the mass publication, *Reader's Digest* in 1945; versions appeared also in the popular *Look* magazine. General Motors even distributed it condensed into a pamphlet.

Hayek, though, declared his commitment to precise definition when he published, "Why I am Not a Conservative," in 1960.[3] This essay made no dent at all in Hayek's American reputation as a conservative, despite its having been republished frequently, most notably in a collection of essays consisting of contributions by conservative thinkers.[4]

Nevertheless, closer analysis reveals that American conservatism often does reflect true conservative elements, especially with regard to social matters. "Conservatives" in the United States tend to rely upon a rhetoric of freedom, which at its base is liberal, but their tendency is to support "freedom" only with regard to economic matters. Application of "freedom" by American conservatives frequently results in lack of freedom for others. They are notorious, for example, for advocating minimal restraints on police conduct (especially with regard to the poor or those of ethnic or racial minorities), for opposing any conduct (especially sexual) of which they disapprove, and for placing the citizenry at great risk—reducing their freedom in a very real sense—by supporting universal availability of firearms. Moreover, they seek to eliminate abortion and strip entirely from all women (or even girls) any decision regarding reproduction—evidently oblivious to the contradiction that this places their bodies under government control, greatly increasing government's coercive power. To put it more graphically, if strict anti-abortion policies are put into effect, any woman, regardless of age, the instant she becomes pregnant, finds her body beyond her control, and subject completely to that of the government.

A Look at Conservatism Through History—

A pair of relatively recent, and controversial, books from among the enormous number of writings on conservatism, may provide insights relevant to this discussion. The intention here is not to contend that these studies—Hirschman's *The Rhetoric of Reaction*, and Robin's *The Reactionary Mind*—present definitive analyses of conservatism. Even less is it to produce a comprehensive analysis of both, or either, of these suggestive works; rather, it is to consider them as encouraging thought on issues that may help to understand conservatism as a phenomenon, and to help explain its popularity—especially among those Americans to whom objectively it would appear to be a clear threat. One caution regarding both works is that in numerous countries, conservatives were in the forefront of the development of social welfare programs. Universal healthcare and social insurance, for example, date all the way back to the very conservative Imperial Germany of the 1880s. Oddly, these books' theses seem to fit the United States rather well, even though American conservatism generally is far less pure than is the tendency elsewhere.

Hirschman scrutinizes some two centuries of reactionary rhetoric, and finds that arguments against reform, or efforts to improve the lot of the majority, remain remarkably similar through time. Those opposing change frequently build their case upon the same three arguments. He identifies the three rhetorical devices as Perversity, Futility, and Jeopardy.

As an illustrative digression, consider, for example, the arguments that conservatives today use to oppose choice of toilet facilities by transsexuals. Their oppositional arguments are hardly different from similar arguments used a half century or so ago by opponents of the proposed Equal Rights Amendment to the U.S. Constitution. Looking back another half century or so before that reveals that the same arguments were flung against advocates for woman suffrage itself. Political rights for women in the early twentieth century inspired the same opposition that it did past the mid-point of the century, and that political and social rights for transsexuals do today. With supreme irony, we find conservatives professing terror that a transsexual might assault a woman inside a toilet facility. At the same time, though, these same "conservatives" enthusiastically voted for and continue to support a man who boasted proudly of his sexual success that resulted from his assaults of women. He said that, since he was a celebrity, they would let him get away with anything. Thus, the key here seems to be something other than the notion of assault, itself, which they find easy to dismiss in order to maintain in power a fellow member of the tribe.

The three theses that Hirschman identified are, of course, related. Reform actions, conservatives argue, inevitably produce results contrary to those intended; they cannot achieve their intended purpose, and in fact they create danger. His comment regarding the Perversity Thesis is relevant to them all three: reactionaries "have been powerfully attracted time and time again by the same form of reasoning..." (p. 35).

In scrutinizing "Conservatism from Edmund Burke to Sarah Palin," Corey Robin in *The Reactionary Mind* finds a pattern similar to the one Hirschman discovered, albeit one that he describes in different terms. "Though it is often claimed," he writes, "that the left stands for equality while the right stands for freedom," this is not really the disagreement. "Historically, the conservative has favored liberty for the higher orders and constraint for the lower orders. What the conservative sees and dislikes in equality, in other words is not a threat to freedom but its extension. For in that extension, he sees a loss of his own freedom" (p. 8). Witness the opposition to requirements that businesses provide to their employees' health insurance that includes coverage for contraception. The opposition to such a requirement is framed as protection of the "religious freedom" of corporations. Thus, conservatives protect the employers' views, but permit them to disregard the views, or the needs, of the employees; even, in fact, to some extent to impose their own standards upon those below them.

American Conservatism and the Republican Party—

The more-or-or-less official vehicle for conservatism in contemporary America has become the Republican Party. This is a relatively recent development. Throughout much of the history of the two-party system in the United States, pragmatism rather than ideology characterized the two major parties. Their goals were similar: to elect their own candidates to office, even those with widely varied ideological positions.

In recent years, though, this has changed. The Democratic Party is the same sprawling, varied, barely organized group that inspired the late humorist Will Rogers nearly a century ago to say that he did not belong to any organized political party—he was a Democrat. To be sure, the party no longer includes those who formed much of its base in the old Solid South—southern reactionaries who insisted on white supremacy. Since Lyndon Johnson signed into law the Civil Rights Act of 1964 and the Voting Rights Act of 1965, those elements transferred on a wholesale basis into the Republican Party.

Other than that change, the Democratic Party has not moved to the left, nor has it become more ideological. No one who understands party politics of the New Deal, the Fair Deal, or the Great Society could honestly maintain otherwise. For the last several elections, however, Republicans have managed to secure their party's nominations by claiming to be "more like Ronald Reagan" than their competitors, and to be "the most conservative" candidate in contention. Hence, they largely have abandoned pragmatism for ideology.

Blowing the Whistle on False Equivalence—

In 2012, two highly respected scholars, Thomas E. Mann of the centrist (formerly liberal) Brookings Institution, and Norman J. Ornstein, of the conservative American Enterprise Institute, brought out a book that was startling, but should not have been. It dealt with an issue that should have been obvious, but virtually no prominent commentator had given any indication of being aware that both parties were not to blame equally for the malfunction of America's political system.

Mann and Ornstein had been known throughout their careers for quality research and caution in their conclusions. They had long been associated with arguments reflecting the approach of, "on the one hand," thus and so—but "on the other hand, there are other arguments."

In this book, however, *It's Even Worse than It* Looks, they threw caution—but not quality—to the wind; they revealed that the emperor had no clothes. They courageously demonstrated with great thoroughness the false equivalence that prevailed throughout the news media and permeated Washington's discourse was undeniably wrong. It simply is not true that "both parties have become more extreme," that "both parties are equally at fault for gridlock," or that "each party is as bad as the other." To say they are really is "political correctness," but could not be recognized as such by those who thunder against "liberals."

The fault is not in our stars, nor in our system. It is in one political party, the Grand Old Party; not the Republican Party of our fathers, but today's Republican Party as bequeathed to us by the Reagan revolution, and especially warped by Newt Gingrich and his successor, "no-holds-barred," political activists.

The original book was *It's Even Worse than It Looks*. The year of the stunning election brought a 2016 edition, *It's Even Worse than It Was*. The book is the same, but with a new Preface, and a new Afterword.

The original book, the authors say, aroused a great deal of controversy, especially when the *Washington Post* published an excerpt under the title, "Let's Just Say It: The Republicans Are The Problem." Obviously, the Republicans disliked that, but so did journalists.

Calling out the Republicans for "using unusual and unprecedent-ed parliamentary tactics and tools to delegitimize outcomes and actors from the other party," and accusing it of "promoting mass obstruction and nullification" may have been perfectly obvious to anyone who would look outside the lens of political correctness, but it was an assertion not to be heard —let alone made—in polite company.

Those in the media have become accustomed to forcing their narratives to fit their presentations of false equivalency (p. xii). Mainstream journalists have been especially careful to demon-strate that they are not partisan. The authors note that they did receive much attention from less timid media figures, such as *The Daily Show*, *PBS Newshour*, Bill Moyers, and NPR. "But," they said, "network news shows, including especially their Sunday talk shows that are the staple of political analysis and discourse for the political class, studiously ignored the book and the thesis—a si-lence that has largely continued until the present day"—that was before the actual election (pp. xii–xiii). The result of all this was that there had been little analytical attention to Donald Trump, the Republican nominee and ultimate victor, despite the huge amount of air time presenting him as entertainment. The media, in fact, rarely even took him seriously as a candidate until he had in fact triumphed.

As an aside, ever since the condemnations of the news media by Vice President Agnew, serving as President Nixon's henchman in attacking the press and television, journalists have been especially reluctant to criticize conservatives, who hit back. They have been far more willing to go after liberals, who tend to be more civil, in order to demonstrate that they themselves, the journalists, are not "biased" (no one should forget the untrue allegations—he had not claimed that he "invented the Internet," for example—about presidential candidate Al Gore, whom reporters simply didn't like, as among other things being a "serial exaggerator," or the sav-age treatment that Maureen Dowd, and even MSNBC directed toward the Clinton administration, and that Dowd, despite her understandable disdain for Trump, was unable to resist continuing on throughout Hillary Clinton's candidacy).

What has happened was "the radicalization of the Republican Party," and it was "given impetus and sustenance by a vast talk radio, cable news, and social media, the modern hypercharged partisan press. These outlets attract and reinforce relatively homogeneous audiences with extreme views. At least as problematic is the traditional or mainstream press that routinely provides evenhanded treatment of the decidedly uneven behavior of the two major parties" (p. xvi). There has been no diminution of the "pattern of false equivalence." The solution will of necessity require, Mann and Ornstein say, "big changes in the Republican Party. And those, in turn, will likely occur only in the face of electoral setbacks" (p. XVII). Although generally anticipated, those certainly were not to come in 2016.

It is not only journalists who retreat from revealing Republican extremes. In the social sciences, one would expect political scientists to be among the forefront in evaluating policy, its effects, and its genesis. Yet very few do so, because they fear that would lose their objectivity, and that would not be "scientific." As I have said elsewhere, "The role that political science tends to play in recent times must be troubling for those of its practitioners whose interests trend toward policy. The inside-the-Beltway mentality that permeates the news media frequently stresses method and process, rather than content. To a large extent, political science reflects similar tendencies."[5]

Certainly, there are exceptions; outstanding exceptions. These include especially the authors of the latter two books under examination here—Thomas E. Mann of Brookings, Norman J. Ornstein of the American Enterprise Institute. Paul Pierson of Berkeley, and Jacob S. Hacker of Yale are distinguished political scientists who, as their books so clearly demonstrate, are extremely active in doing what students of government for so long considered it their duty to do: speaking truth to power (see chapter 3).

Hacker was quite instrumental also with regard to the crafting of healthcare reform. He did say his universities had treated him always very well, but had to point out that policy advocacy is not well regarded within the discipline. The reason for this, he said, might seem to be obvious, because "policy recommendations seem to be a breach of objectivity and a distraction from real scholarship." Regardless, he said, such rigidity does not characterize every discipline. "Economists routinely engage with public issues while political scientists appear more reticent."[6] Political scientists, in fact, have been known occasionally to go so far— so absurdly far—as to demand that others of their discipline not identify themselves as political scientists when speaking out on public issues.

The more one considers the range of recent political developments, though, the more difficult it is to make the case that Trump burst on the scene from the outside as a disruptor. Whether or not he could have been predicted (and certainly, by most observers including this one he was not), he seems actually to have been an outgrowth of conservative policies, a culmination of the policies that preceded him. Goldwater, Nixon, and Reagan—and one must admit, also, George Wallace, who was not a Republican— provided the foundation. The post-Reagan Republican Party with its conservative ideologues and their activists (including Newt Gingrich, Tom DeLay, Dick, Cheney, and Mitch McConnell) built steadily upon that foundation. Trump is not a doctrinaire conservative; he does not have to be one to be the logical conclusion of the policies that the conservatives have crafted and installed. To appreciate this, it is helpful to consider the history of the "Grand Old Party," or GOP.

Reaching for Power Beyond the Pale—

As American conservatives cast off restraints in their efforts to secure power, the last few decades have seen them regularly proceed
beyond the boundaries of politics as usual. They forced a recall
election in 2003 for Gray Davis, recently re-elected as governor
of California, and forced him from office. They worked openly to
create opposition to essential elements of American government,
such as when, under a plan designed by Representative Newt Gingrich, they alleged in 1992 a "banking scandal" in the U.S. House
of Representatives (where members had set up a sort of credit
union with their own funds, and in which no money was lost, and
no public money was even involved). The goal was to bring criticism to Congress as an institution, thus generating public hostility
to incumbent members and giving advantage to Republican chal-
lengers. In Texas, they worked to gain control of the state's legislature in order to re-draw the boundaries of congressional districts
even though the boundaries had just been drawn to accommodate
findings from the 2000 census. The purpose was to elect five additional Republicans to the U.S. House. In a solely political move, in
December 1998, the lame-duck House impeached a sitting Democratic president, Bill Clinton, albeit failing in February 1999 to
gain a conviction (or even a majority against him, let alone the
two thirds required to convict) in the U.S. Senate. As the minority party in the U.S. Senate, the Republicans so institutionalized
the filibuster—a procedure that previously had been quite rare—
that it became routine. The new reality was that "bills require 60
votes to pass the Senate" (60 votes are required to halt debate, and
break a filibuster). As the Senate's majority party, they refused
compromises with the Democratic president, Barack Obama, and
sought to make his defeat, not sound policies for the country, their
"number-one priority." They refused even to hold hearings for an
Obama nominee to the Supreme Court, although many had identified that nominee as someone they could support. The result
was that they held the vacancy open for nearly a year, violating all
precedent, in order to prevent a Democratic president from filling

the seat. Despite their allegations, this had never happened before. With a straight face, they say "the people have spoken" to support the appointment of a conservative on the Supreme Court, despite the nearly three million popular vote majority who chose Secretary Clinton. They also ignore the Constitution, which shields the federal judiciary from popular control.

Senator McConnell, who was the architect of the unprecedented theft of a seat on the Supreme Court, subsequently chortled that it was the proudest moment of his political career. Lest anyone believe that this was "politics as usual," or that "both parties do it," consider that the Democrats in 1973, as described in Chapter 4, actually had an opportunity to steal the presidency itself. They declined to do so, however, because it would not have been honorable. No such consideration has ever halted today's most zealous conservatives in their pursuit of power. They would deride it as foolish.

As for the stolen Supreme Court seat, some Republicans even urged that the seat be kept open for four, or possibly eight, years, should Hillary Clinton be the new president. It is clear that drivers of the Republican Party have become ideologues; it was made equally clear when, for ideological reasons, they openly sought to make duly-passed and implemented programs fail, rather than to make them work as well as possible for the country's good.

These, and numerous other actions, were certainly out of the mainstream. However, they were not illegal. For the most part, although they were rough and uncivil politics, they generally did not constitute direct attacks on the constitutional system itself. The same cannot be said for other actions that clearly transgressed the boundaries of the acceptable; actions that they would be quick to label "treasonous," if they had been committed by their opponents. A review of some of these should be illustrative of the effects of conservative ideological principles as practiced by America's movement conservatives.

"Watergate," the assault on American constitutional procedures that ultimately forced President Richard Nixon from office is too well known to need extensive discussion here. It was certainly extreme, and it led to the only presidential resignation to date. Other, later, actions though, appear to have been more extreme even than Watergate.

One of those also dealt with Nixon. It now is well known, even beyond scholars, that Nixon's agents worked to sabotage the Paris peace talks that had been scheduled in 1968. Nixon feared that a peace agreement would work in favor of Vice President Hubert Humphrey, who was his opponent in the presidential race. President Johnson became aware of these actions—actions that may well have prolonged the war, with its death and destruction—but Nixon fervently denied any knowledge, and said that he could not in good conscience have done such a thing. LBJ did not have solid proof, so he did not go public, and Nixon was elected. Nixon, of course, may have won in any case, and the government of South Vietnam might have boycotted the Paris talks even without the Nixon administration's urging, but the election was so close that anything might have made a difference.

Regardless, in 2007, the Nixon Library opened the notes of top Nixon aide, H. R. Haldeman, and those notes were unequivocal. Nixon not only knew, he ordered directly that the peace talks be "monkey wrenched." Recently, John A. Farrell, who was working on a Nixon biography, found the notes, and wrote of "Nixon's Vietnam Treachery," in a *New York Times* op ed piece.[7] In a conversation with President Johnson, Republican minority leader Senator Everett Dirksen agreed with the president that the action had been "treasonous."[8]

There have been persistent, but unproved, allegations that agents of Ronald Reagan did something similar in 1980, to prevent an "October surprise" release of the American hostages held in Iran before the election. The allegation is that the Iranians were promised arms if they were to delay release so long as President Carter remained in office. The charges originated from Gary Sick, who was an official with the National Security Council in the Carter administration,[9] although there have been other works on the subject. Sick concedes that there is no clear evidence of guilt, no "smoking gun," but he argues that there is a strong circumstantial case based on his computer analyses of a database regarding arms transfers. President Carter, himself, "not one to make reckless charges,"[10] has suggested that Sick's allegations may be correct. "In October 1991, the Senate voted to conduct an inquiry, but the next month, Senate Republicans were able to block funding for it."[11] There is no direct evidence; there is only knowledge that President Reagan, in a puzzling move, did provide arms to Iranian groups that would then use them against the United States; that Senate Republicans did refuse to permit an investigation; and that Nixon agents had done something similar. Thus, this should not be considered as definitive, but it is plausible.

It also is certainly a possibility. We do know that despite President Reagan's clear statement that he would never negotiate with terrorists, his administration later did just that, resulting in the "Iran-Contra" scandal. Moreover, the result of Iran-Contra was that the government of the United States actually provided arms to the forces that were using them against Americans. There is little doubt what conservatives would have said if Presidents Clinton or Obama had done the same. They would not have hesitated to scream "Treason!".

During the administration of George W. Bush, Ambassador Joseph Wilson wrote that he found no evidence of Iraqi purchase of nuclear materials in Africa when he journeyed there to conduct a search. Angry at this contradiction of President Bush's statements, officials from Vice President Cheney's office retaliated by leaking the name of Wilson's wife, Valerie Plame Wilson, who was an undercover agent of the CIA. This destroyed her career. It could have endangered her life, and certainly damaged the United States by undercutting the work she was doing. Conservatives later made much of Hillary Clinton's use of a private server for emails, but this earlier situation was an instance of deliberate actions taken against American interests. Mrs. Clinton's situation, at worst, was careless; neither dangerous nor vindictive. In an ironic twist, numerous officials of the Trump administration now are known to use private servers for their official emails, but conservatives seem not to be concerned when it is a Trump official, and not Hillary Clinton, who is the offender.

During the Obama administration, 47 Republican senators in March 2015 signed a letter inspired by Senator Tom Cotton, of Arkansas, to the Iranian leadership. The signers of the letter talked down to the Iranian leaders, purporting to school them on the details of the U.S. Constitution. They urged Iran's leaders to ignore the president of the United States, who was negotiating a nuclear agreement with them. Dealing directly with a foreign power to undercut the foreign policy of a sitting president is not acceptable, and would have created outrage if done by Democrats against a Republican president.

Similarly, Republican House speaker, John Boehner, invited the head of government of a foreign nation to address a joint session of Congress in order to undercut President Obama's Iran policy, and deliberately withheld information of the invitation from the president. The foreign leader, Israel's Benyamin Netanyahu, accepted, unwisely, and came to the United States, where he delivered his address. Reuters put it this way:

> House Speaker John Boehner's annoyance with President Barack Obama is turning into a grudge match against the Constitution.

> Boehner's decision to invite a foreign head of government to address Congress without first consulting the sitting president has no precedent in American history. And for a simple reason. It's unconstitutional.

Boehner (R-Ohio) fully admits that his failure to communicate with the White House was not an oversight. Like a schoolboy passing notes when the teacher turns to the blackboard, he sneaked behind Obama's back to set the date for Israeli Prime Minister Benjamin Netanyahu's speech with his country's ambassador to the United States. Boehner asked the foreign dignitary not to tell the U.S. president.

"I wanted to make sure," Boehner later explained on Fox News, "there was no interference." Netanyahu is now scheduled to address a joint session of Congress on March 3 (Cobbs 2015).

In case these examples are insufficient, there are more. It now is clear that the Russians involved themselves in American elections in 2016, with intent to damage the presidential prospects of the Democratic candidate, Hillary Clinton, and advance those of the Republican candidate, Donald Trump. To be sure, the United States has been guilty of similar meddling abroad, so there is little excuse for outrage against the Russians. This is what they do.

What should be source for outrage, though, is that during his campaign, the Republican candidate openly called for Russian interference. It may have been phrased as a joke, but that sort of joke is not one that a presidential candidate should be permitted to make. Mr. Trump called for interference—and there was interference.

Trump also made numerous calls for the imprisonment of his opponent. This, for obvious reasons, is far beyond the boundaries of acceptable conduct in American politics. He also made references, not very veiled, to the need for violence if the election did not go his way. Peaceful elections and peaceful changes of power are one of the great strengths of the American political system, and have been a beneficial example to world political practice. To have a presidential candidate—and a successful one at that—speak against such traditions is enormously dangerous.

American Conservatives and Social Programs—

It should be clear by now that conservative principles are incompatible with social programs. This should come as no surprise, because apart from a rhetorical commitment to "freedom," conservatives' primary goal is to reduce government spending (not to mention the ability of the government to affect the economy, or to regulate private power holders). The primacy of such a goal may be appropriate for a business in order to secure profits; a government, however, especially government in a democracy, has as its first order of business the safety *and also the welfare* of its citizens. Economy is an appropriate goal, but only if consistent with the public good. When economy comes to the forefront and supersedes other goals, as conservatives would have it, governmental services suffer. When governmental services suffer, so does its effectiveness, and so do the citizens.

Many congressional Republicans have been notorious for their desire to "reform" Social Security by cutting benefits, or by eliminating the system through privatization. They have openly scorned Medicare. Mick Mulvany, the current budget director for Mr. Trump, has suggested the elimination of Social Security Disability Benefits, signed into law by a Republican president, Dwight Eisenhower. Mulvany has said that he cannot support a program such as Meals on Wheels for elderly and disabled homebound, which he described as only "sounding good," but not really justified. The budget proposal in general envisions drastic cuts for nearly every governmental program, great tax reductions for the wealthy, but increased funding for the military and for border control.

Thus, whatever strengths conservative principles may have, they do not include improving the lot of the poor, or even of anyone else, below the most privileged. Based on their preferences, it would seem as though conservatives would scoff at the notion that a society may be evaluated by the manner in which it treats the least of us.

The Futility Thesis Turned Toward American Conservatism—

Whatever strengths conservative principles may offer, they do not seem to include success in practice. Often, they cannot be implemented; when implemented, the result at best fails to meet their expectations. Whenever conservatives manage to elect one of their own, they face disappointment. Even the heralded Ronald Reagan was not immune. He promised to trim the number of cabinet departments by eliminating the Departments of Education and Energy. Not only did he fail to do so, he added another, Veterans' Affairs. He promised to balance budgets. Not only did he fail ever even to submit a balanced budget to Congress, he ran up the greatest deficits in history to that time. What he did accomplish was to aggravate the traditional American skepticism of government into a strongly anti-government mentality that has made it even more difficult to have the best government. Enshrining hostility to government and to regulation does not bring improvements. Those old enough to remember the Reagan administration will remember the disappointment of conservatives. They could not attack Reagan directly, considering his status as patron saint of the party, which made him at least somewhat immune, but the persistent cry was directed to his aides: "let Reagan be Reagan!" his partisans demanded. Never mind that this did not say much for their view of his independent judgment.

"Much of this history has been forgotten or forgiven by the Right in the haze of idolatry that envelopes Reagan. But in 1988, libertarian scholar Sheldon Richman summed up the far-right's disenchantment in an essay titled 'The Sad Legacy of Ronald Reagan.' He noted, 'The number of free-market achievements by the administration are so few that they can be counted on one hand—with fingers left over.'"[12]

Reagan's successor, the first George Bush, had said during the campaign, "read my lips—no new taxes," giving in to the growing hostility among Republicans against taxation. As president, however, Mr. Bush recognized that a tax increases were necessary. His broken pledge reflected his concern for good government, but his constituents were outraged at his "betrayal."

The next conservative activist in the presidency was George W. Bush. His time in office offended his constituents, because they saw him as an advocate of "big government," despite his efforts to reduce regulation and his drastic reduction in taxes.

When President Clinton raised taxes, there were dire cries of doom. The taxes would bring ruin to the economy. What followed, though, was great prosperity. It was the George W. Bush tax *reductions* that were followed by the greatest economic calamity since the Great Depression.

The conservative answer to all this is that these conservatives did not succeed (except that they cannot criticize Reagan, so they romanticize him) for one reason: they were not conservative enough. Governor Bobby Jindal's conservative policies left his state of Louisiana a disaster. When Governor Sam Brownback of Kansas (where I live) embarked upon his great experiment, and slashed taxes, the state's economy became a basket case. Brownback still cannot admit it, saying that the great benefits he predicted only need more time to come. His guru Arthur Laffer insists that the enormous tax cuts were simply not large enough. Vice President Pence, as governor of Indiana, "proclaimed in 2014 that Indiana was 'blazing a trail for low taxes, balanced budgets and economic freedom in the Midwest.' In truth, Indiana was blazing a trail to the bottom. The state's poverty rate rose by more than one third from 2007 to 2013, and the median household income declined nearly 11 percent. Indiana performed worse than any neighboring state on both counts."[13] The neighboring states of Wisconsin and Minnesota share many similarities, and can be taken as excellent examples of the effects of conservative policies. It is well known that Wisconsin, under the conservative, anti-union, administration of Governor Scott Walker, has suffered in education, public health, public investment, and in general has declined as a result of Walker's ideological "economic freedom" policies. Immediately to the west, however, during the same period, Minnesota has implemented liberal policies and has thrived. California offers another recent example of the success of liberal policies.

And so it goes. Conservatives have their ideology. When applied, it fails. Their solution is always more of the same. When in a hole, dig faster! The result is disaster for the people.

Notes

1 Adapted from an earlier version that appeared in *Poverty and Public Policy* 9 (2) (September 2016).

2 Friedrich A. Hayek, *The Road to Serfdom* (Chicago, IL: University of Chicago Press, 1944).

3 Friedrich A. Hayek, "Why I Am Not a Conservative." *The Constitution of Liberty* (Chicago, IL: University of Chicago Press, 1960). Frank S. Meyer, *What Is Conservatism?* (New York: Holt, Rinehart, and Winston, 1967).

4 Meyer, *What Is Conservatism?*, 88–103.

5 Max J. Skidmore, "'Bipartisanship' as a Detriment to Anti-Poverty Efforts: Some Contrarian Comments," *Poverty and Public Policy* 5 (3) (September 2013).

6 Quoted *ibid.*

7 John A. Farrell, "Nixon's Vietnam Treachery," *New York Times* (January 1, 2017), p. SR9. See also Max J. Skidmore, *Presidential Politics* (Jefferson, NC: McFarland, 2004), 288; and Robert M. Dallek, *Flawed Giant: Lyndon Johnson and His Times, 1961–1973* (New York: Oxford University Press, 1998), 618–619; Farrell's excellent biography has now been published: *Richard Nixon: The Life* (New York: Doubleday, 2017).

8   John A. Farrell, *Nixon: The Life* (New York: Doubleday, 2017), 342–343.

9   Gary Sick, *October Surprise: America's Hostages in Iran and the Election of Ronald Reagan* (New York: Crown, 1991).

10 Skidmore, 311–312.

11 Burton I. Kaufman, *The Presidency of James Earl Carter, Jr.* (Lawrence: The University Press of Kansas, 1993), 213–214.

12 Quoted in, Theo Anderson, (2017). "The Right-Wing Machine Behind the Curtain," *In These Times* (April 2017), 15.

13 *Ibid.,* 17.

CHAPTER 3
SHINING LIGHT ON DARK POLITICS:
AN ESSAY AND REVIEW[1]

Steven Hill (2016), *Expand Social Security Now! How to Ensure Americans Get the Retirement They Deserve,* Boston: Beacon Press. $15.00, pp. 178, pbk. ISBN 978-0-8070-2843-8.

Jane Mayer (2016), *Dark Money: The Hidden History of the Billionaires Behind the Rise of the Radical Right,* New York: Doubleday. $29.95, pp. 450, hdbk. ISBN 978-0-385-53559-5.

Jacob S. Hacker and Paul Pierson (2016), *American Amnesia: How the War on Government Led Us to Forget What Made America Prosper,* New York: Simon and Schuster. $28.00, pp. 455, hdbk. ISBN 978-1-4516-6782-0.

Ari Rabin-Havt and Media Matters (2016), *Lies, Incorporated: The World of Post-Truth Politics,* New York: Anchor Books. $15.00, pp. 238, pbk. ISBN 978-0-307-27959-0.

Introduction—

Against every dictate of reason, the most successful government program in the history of the United States, the one most favored and most strongly supported by the citizenry, and the one that as a fortunate by-product is the greatest anti-poverty program Americans have ever experienced has endured decades of lavishly financed attacks. That program is Social Security, and one may throw in Medicare—another enormously successful and equally beloved program—as well.

As astonishing as the attacks on social insurance in the United States are, they are only a portion of the "dark politics" that funds from some of the country's richest citizens have created. One must concede that these ultra-wealthy have proceeded carefully, and skillfully.

Throughout the extended analysis that follows, the reader will note something rare outside of partisan politics: sharp criticisms of many of today's Republican officeholders. As will be explained, however, this cannot be avoided without leaving the analysis incomplete or misleading.

These criticisms are not intended to be partisan. Rather, they reflect the effect of powerful interests that have taken over the modern Republican Party, and have carried it far from its heritage of democratic conservatism. The criticisms are not to be taken as condemnation of the Republican Party as an entity, but of the extremist forces that have diverted it from its mainstream roots, and invested it with a "rule or ruin" ideology that is accurately described by the slang phrase, "my way or the highway." In fact, many committed Republicans have gone public with similar comments critical of their own party's descent into the ideological abyss.

The four books under examination here contain themes that are some of the most highly relevant to questions of poverty in the United States, and they fit together superbly to put forth a comprehensive picture of much that plagues American politics today. They warrant extended consideration, as do the varied strains of American politics that are influential with regard to American poverty, broadly conceived. *Poverty and Public Policy* is one of the few journals that is able to devote sufficient space to give these books, and other relevant themes, their due.

This essay, in fact, is more than a review, even an extended review. It proceeds from these four books under examination to add its own insights, conclusions, and recommendations. As the communication scholar Joey Skidmore (my son) has recognized, reviews can themselves arise to a qualitatively different creative form, apart from and in addition to the material under review.[2]

Historically, Republicans and Democrats as a rule have fought one another, but have worked together to compromise for the good of the country. Each party seeks to have its programs enacted, and perhaps even to repeal programs it opposes. Only recently, though, and only within one party, has it become routine to filibuster to achieve every possible goal, and to work to sabotage enacted programs hoping to make them fail, regardless of the effects that might have on the country or its people. Instead of working together to make any program perform as well as possible, that party now is ideologically driven to undermine whatever it opposes.

The same impetus is seen in attempts by Republicans across the country to suppress the vote. At an otherwise excellent Chautauqua program in May 2016, one speaker on contemporary politics criticized "gridlock," but his objection to gridlock came essentially because it prevented achievement of a "Grand Bargain," to reduce government spending. Most in the elderly audience would likely have reacted adversely had they recognized that "Grand Bargain" is a euphemism for severely reducing—if not entirely eliminating—Social Security and Medicare. Similarly, a more sophisticated audience would probably have known that spending is not, as the speaker put it, out of control. Nor would they have accepted the notion that the adoption of additional austerity policies under current circumstances would be beneficial, but would recognize that they would be economically quite harmful.

When one audience member asked about voter suppression, the speaker, seeking to be even-handed, resorted to the most egregious tactic, false equivalency. He replied, "well, both sides do it, but recently, the Republicans may have done it a little more." "Little more," indeed.

That, of course, is absurd. To be sure, both parties attempt to maximize their turnout and the effects of their supporters' votes, and both have been guilty of gerrymandering. In modern American politics, however, only the Republicans have openly created roadblocks to voting, and only they have sought deliberately to make voting as difficult as possible, thus hampering the basic exercise of the most fundamental democratic right of qualified citizens. They recognize that lower turnouts generally favor them, because they reduce participation by the poor, by racial, ethnic, and other minorities, and by the less politically engaged.

The purposes that motivate the architects of dark politics are primarily twofold: the one selfish, and the other ideological (although these are related). From the selfish impulse, they have sought successfully to reduce taxation across the board. Of course, they are concerned with paying the minimum, but beyond that they are working diligently to "starve the beast." That is, whenever possible they seek to deny to government the funds it requires to operate, so that it will be too impotent to imposes regulations upon them. The power of the state, they believe, should lie with them, and not with the representatives of the people. Therein is the ideological justification for their exercise of power: they attempt, wherever possible, to weaken or eliminate those programs designed to improve people's lives. They maintain a romantic fancy of a ruggedly individualistic country in which the strong survive and prosper, while the rest defer to their betters, and accept their deprived lot. It is irrelevant that much of what they perceive as strength comes from inherited wealth, from lucrative government contracts, or otherwise benefiting from good fortune, rather than from inherent strength.

All this they do in the name of "freedom." This demonstrates that one should be wary of anyone who loudly professes to be defending freedom, when the freedom defended would deprive others of their own freedom to act. The freedom the wealthy manipulators seek is for themselves only, and would restrict, not enhance, the freedom of others. Examples include, but certainly are not limited to, those who seek "religious freedom" to deny their employees certain rights, or the strained doctrine embraced by the Supreme Court that equates spending money with freedom of speech, thus overtly destroying any semblance of equality. It should be apparent that, among other things, terrible state budgetary troubles, declining levels of public services, hostility toward government, irrationality in politics, and a willingness to disregard the "rules of the game" to achieve partisan ends all are accumulating results of the politics of the 1980s, and of the "Reagan Revolution."

Shifts in Consensus on Social Security—

The attacks on Social Security generally have been done in such a manner as to avoid appearing as attacks. Rather, they have masqueraded as support for the program, and have cynically purported only to be recommending necessary "reforms." These always took the form of benefit cuts or privatization, justified with allegations that the system had become "unsustainable." So carefully were the attacks crafted that none but a few of us recognized that they were based on ideology, not economics. Therefore, few people recognized what was going on, so that over a period of decades, a conventional wisdom developed that questioned the very basis of the most successful program of economic security in history.

This distorted view, this new conventional wisdom, reflected the skill of the architects of those who crafted the attack narrative. It had bipartisan effects. Most Democrats—at least for a time—came to accept the scenario of Social Security as "unsustainable," unless "reformed," joining with virtually all Republicans. The differences between them tended to be of degree only: Republicans were far more likely to advance draconian policies that at best would convert the vital social programs into means-tested "welfare" schemes, while at worst would eliminate them altogether. Either approach would destroy contributory social insurance.

More conservative Democrats tended to hope simply for benefit reductions, but some actually agreed with the Republican attackers. Large numbers of those in both parties had come to accept the idea that Social Security had to be "saved." The story of how this came about now has been told by several writers. In any event, the opponents' façade began to crack in the late 1990s, when various scholars began to demonstrate that Social Security was sound after all, and that the charges against it at best were misrepresentations, and at worst were overtly false.

In 2011, in the pages of *Poverty and Public Policy*, I discussed a dozen such works dating back to 1997.[3] These included in chronological order, books by Kingson and Shulz, *Social Security in the 21st Century* (1997); Robert Eisner, *Social Security: MORE, not Less* (1998); by me, *Social Security and Its Enemies*; by Baker and Weisbrot, *Social Security: The Phony Crisis* (both 1999); by Benavie, *Social Security under the Gun*; by White, *False Alarm: Why the Greatest Threat to Social Security and Medicare Is the Campaign to "Save" Them* (both 2003); by Béland, *Social Security: History and Politics from the New Deal to the Privatization Debate*; by Hiltzik, *The Plot Against Social Security*; and by Altman, *The Battle for Social Security* (all 2005); by me, *Securing America's* Future; by Ghilarducci, *When I'm Sixty-Four: The Plot Against Pensions and the Plan to Save Them*; and by DeWitt et al., *Social Security: A Documentary History* (all 2008). Eric Laursen's massive, and excellent, *People's Pension*, came out in 2012, too late to be included, but I reviewed it in a separate piece, also in this journal, under the title "Social Security and Its Discontents."[4]

Happily, the consensus began to shift dramatically. The conversation changed so much that the opponents found themselves facing more than a backlash that identified their errors. More and more authorities were beginning to recognize that Social Security, far from needing benefit cuts, actually required expansion. Nancy Altman and Eric Kingson in 2010 formed their fine organization, Social Security Works, to support the system and work to broaden and increase its benefits.

The momentum continued to gather, and Steven Hill brought forth his own powerful argument describing the importance of expanding Social Security. Moreover, he suggested a plausible method by which it may be accomplished. That his message is no longer that of a solitary figure crying into the wind is indicated by the fact that "with Democratic senators Warren and Sanders leading the way, 43 out of 100 U.S. senators and 116 out of 435 House members have gone on record in favor of expansion, as have leading progressive economists like Paul Krugman and Dean Baker" (p. 76). Fortunately, after Hill wrote, Democratic presidential aspirant Hillary Clinton joined Sanders, Warren, and the others to support expansion. President Obama, early in his presidency, had appeared to be somewhat receptive to calls for a "Grand Bargain," and to be sure, Social Security was not featured prominently in his administration. As his administration ended, though, Obama had joined the growing chorus of voices calling for expansion. Unfortunately, Donald Trump's electoral college win meant that the Democrats' momentum could not be made policy for some years yet.

Hill's analysis recognized that since the Reagan era, there have been attempts "to unravel key cornerstones of the New Deal," that have included "extreme deregulation" of the banking and financial industry. These, he notes, contributed substantially to the 2008 economic collapse. Given such approaches, it was to have been expected that "the architects of austerity have also waged a war to undercut Social Security" (p. 49).

He summarized the bipartisan nature of the attacks on Social Security, and was explicitly critical of presidential aspirant Hillary Clinton for what he took to be equivocation regarding attempts at "reform"—too critical, actually, considering the firm support she provided for the system as her campaign progressed—although he did remark that she said the Republican efforts to undermine Social Security were simply wrong (p. 58). He noted the skill of the Republicans at staying "on message," and at re-defining terms to make them fit their anti-Social-Security agenda. They continually stressed such things as debt and deficits, while nonetheless urging enormous tax reductions. They maintained rigid discipline over their vocabulary, such as never referring to inheritance or estate taxes, but flinging around their newly minted jargon term, the dreaded "death tax" (pp. 50–51).

Key to his discussion was an examination of the anti-Social Security zealot, billionaire Peter G. Peterson, who was instrumental in creating such opposition organizations as the Concord Coalition, the "Fix the Debt" campaign, the Committee for a Responsible Federal Budget, and most important, "his very own Peter G. Peterson Foundation" (which he launched in 2008). He financed this foundation with one BILLION dollars of his own funds, and explicitly charged it with undermining the public's confidence in Social Security (p. 53).

One of Peterson's activities was to organize "a charade of town hall meetings to advance his agenda." His foundation, Hill says, "reportedly gave over $2 million to America Speaks, one of the leading innovators in the field of public deliberative democracy, to organize nineteen town hall meetings across the country." Participants came together to deliberate on "the debt problem," and found themselves faced with forced choices, after having received biased material that was passed off as "objective" information regarding problems and solutions. Enough information was available in advance to alert progressives to participate, and the result was widespread outcomes far different from those intended. The Los Angeles meeting, for example, wound up supporting additional taxes on the wealthy, as "these Americans spoke, loudly and clearly, about their opposition to rolling back Social Security and Medicare" (pp. 55–56). Such results were not unique to Los Angeles, and were duplicated elsewhere. Similar results occurred in the meeting in the Kansas City metropolitan area, where I attended as a participant, and subsequently produced a detailed analysis of the proceedings.[5]

The entire "Town Hall" meeting program vanished. In fact, the "AmericaSpeaks" organization itself disbanded a few months after the Peterson fiasco. Perhaps the unintended outcomes rejecting austerity were partly responsible.

Hill began with an excellent, and extended, discussion of the nature of the attacks on Social Security. He also made clear just what is at stake for the American people in the struggle. The original Act of 1935 provided only retirement benefits.

With the 1939 Amendments, the Act came to include protection for wives (later this became husbands, as well) of retirees—who also had lost income because of the age of the wage-earner the husband. Additionally, it brought under coverage survivors who had lost wages because of the death of the wage earners: widows (later, widowers also), and minor children.

Hill devoted an entire chapter to "The Collapse of the Three-Legged Stool" (chapter 2), a metaphor that conventional wisdom generally accepts as dating from the program's origin (one leg is Social Security, a second is personal savings and investment, and the third is company pensions). In a forthcoming work, however, Nancy Altman demonstrates that the metaphor came into being as conservative forces sought to misrepresent Social Security as never having been intended to be a full retirement system.[6] She provides full documentation to explode the generally accepted view of the metaphor. In any case, Hill cites "pensions and employer-retirement plans" as "the first failing leg of retirement security" (p. 30). Certainly, companies and other employers are increasingly withdrawing from any obligation they may have felt to offer pensions to their employees. Many of those that remain no longer are "defined benefit" plans, but rather "defined contribution" plans that relieve the employer of any responsibility to provide a given level of benefits, and place all risk upon the employees. At the same time that many employers had begun to complain that they could no longer afford to provide defined-benefit pensions, they were "paying increasingly astronomical salaries and bonus packages to their executives" (p. 35).

Although the majority of public employees still have retirement systems, they, along with their counterparts in the private sector, now often face difficulties. Retirement plans across the economy have been troubled by the retirement of baby boomers that had been anticipated all along, but also by the erratic, and often very poor, performance of investments in the first years of the twenty-first century through at least 2008. What has been truly reprehensible, though, "was that some public and private pension plans failed to make adequate contributions into their funds, despite making hefty promises to employees, irresponsibly spending employees' contributions on other priorities. Ultimately many private and public pension funds became plagued by inadequate funding and threats of bankruptcy" (p. 31).

The second "failing leg" of the three that presumably were to hold up the stool of retirement income was all that the worker had managed to accumulate personally, primarily investments and equity in the home. The Great Recession took care of the demolition of that leg. The amounts consumers owe on credit cards are enormous, and exacerbated by rates of interest far above those elsewhere in the economy (except for those charged in the thriving—and egregious—payday loan industry). Until fairly recently, these credit-card rates would never have been permitted under the law. They greatly exceed those formerly outlawed universally as usury.

Thus, regardless of the misconception that Social Security had not been designed to be a full retirement system, it is clear that for the vast majority of workers it is all that they will have. Despite that, it remains under serious attack. Hill points out, correctly, that it adds not a penny to the federal deficit. Moreover, he notes, regardless of the scare propaganda, Social Security is not "going broke" (pp. 46–47). He could have gone further, and demonstrated that efforts to reduce the deficit by cutting benefits would have no effect whatever on the deficit and would simply build up greater trust funds. The only way to reduce the deficit by lowering benefits would be to change the law so that workers would still pay in, but their payments would be diverted away from benefits toward deficit reduction. That is, workers would be required to bear the burden of austerity in order to protect the vast fortunes of the ultra wealthy by keeping their taxes extraordinarily low. He could also have argued that it is impossible for Social Security to be "bankrupt," or "go broke." Even if the trust funds were completely gone, there still would be tax money coming in to pay benefits. At the worst, there would be benefit reductions, but the amounts paid out would still be greater than they are currently.

Hill described the lunacy of cutting Social Security when it is the only component of the country's retirement system that remains unimpaired. He says, on the contrary, that "we should *double* [*sic*] the individual payout for the 43 million Americans who annually receive individual retirement benefits" (p. 47). He describes a plausible way in which this could be done, but first he helps Americans recognize that much of what is said about Social Security is simply a lie.

There are nine such lies that he identifies. The first is that Social Security is going broke, and will bankrupt the country. We already have seen that this is false. In fact, so long as America maintains control of its own currency and pays its bills in dollars, it is impossible for it to have too few dollars than it needs. The second charge is that we will have progressively fewer workers for each beneficiary. For many reasons, some quite technical, this is untrue. It is true that retirement of baby boomers at its peak will add benefit recipients, and that the populace is growing older, at least for now. Nevertheless, the rush of women into the work force has meant that at the height of the boomer retirement, there still will be a greater proportion of the population in the work force than there was in 1965, when all was well with Social Security.

The third lie is that everyone would do better by investing on his or her own than by relying on Social Security. Some people certainly would, but most would not, and some would lose every-thing. There are a number of things such an argument overlooks. Very few people are skilled at investment, and studies indicate that even professionals often do not do very well. Moreover, the argument concerns only retirement, and ignores the spousal benefits of Social Security, its disability coverage, its survivors' benefits, and the protection against inflation that its benefits provide—they grow to keep pace with inflation, and they last a lifetime. One who lives a long time can outlive private benefits, but retirement benefits from Social Security lasts as long as the beneficiaries themselves. Anyone who still believes 401k investments inevitably are better than Social Security should consider that all those Enron employees who poured their funds into 401k plans, lost them entirely. They still have their Social Security coverage. The fourth lie Hill discusses is that Social Security steals from the young, saddles them with debt, and creates generational unfairness. Much of this comes from the ever-present Pete Peterson. It is wrong. Social Security benefits young workers by providing them with disability coverage, and young dependents by providing them with life insurance on their wage-earning parents. Additionally, by enabling many older people to live independently, Social Security relieves many of the young of obligations to provide direct support to their parents and grandparents. Actually, nearly a third of Social Security's benefit checks go to people younger than retirement age. Hill's fifth lie is that the retirement age needs to be raised. This would be an enormous benefit reduction, and would cause great hardship, especially on those who earn the least.

Allegations of troubles with the disability program constitute Hill's sixth lie. Republicans and some journalists have made much of a presumed rush to claim disability benefits from people so simply "don't want to work." As he points out, most people who become disabled have been earning about $42,000 per year, while disability checks bring only about $14,000 (p. 93). That would be a bad trade. The truth, though, is that Social Security Disability benefits are notoriously difficult to get. The disability must be severe. Almost everyone who files for disability benefits is rejected, and has to appeal, often numerous times. Overall, more than half of those who seek to obtain SSDI never manage to qualify. That is the scandal, not the imagined hordes of able-bodied, but lazy, people who milk the system.

The final three allegations that Hill dispels deal with charges of "socialism" that doesn't fit American values, that Social Security is overly generous and America cannot afford it, and that the system was designed for an earlier time, and so by definition, it cannot meet today's needs (pp. 92–101). These are simply silly. Whatever label one wishes to apply to Social Security is irrelevant. Study after study demonstrates that it is among the most popular programs in American history, if not the most popular. It is demonstrably less generous than those of many other countries, none of which has the economic strength of the United States. Finally, it continues to succeed in keeping large numbers of Americans from sinking into poverty. Most retirees get a substantial portion of their income from its benefits, and about a fifth of them have no other income at all. The date the program was designed is irrelevant, since it continues to function very well.

That is not to say that it cannot be improved, and Hill outlines a way. Social Security's greatest flaw, he notes, is that it pays too little, not too much. He suggests doubling benefits by crafting an expansion that he calls "Social Security Plus." This could be done in various ways, he says, but he recommends several revisions to the tax code that could provide more money to the trust funds, as well as lifting the cap on the amount of wages subject to FICA (Social Security taxes). Currently, the rate is 6.2% of an employee's salary, matched by the employer's contribution of the same amount, but only up to wages of $127,200 per year, at which point the taxable wages are capped, and there is no tax above that amount.

For Social Security Plus, Hill would provide a "new universal flat benefit, Social Security B, funded by various mechanisms other than a payroll tax" (p. 120). This scheme would be reminiscent of Medicare, which has several parts, in addition to Part A, the basic hospitalization benefits paid for through a payroll tax, as Social Security is. For Medicare, the cap on taxable wages was removed years ago. The 1.45% Medicare tax (matched by the employer) already is applied to the employee's full salary. Of course, Hill would provide an overall cap on benefits, so that no one person would receive an enormous payment each month under any circumstances.

Hill's book is excellent. He provides needed corrections to many misconceptions regarding Social Security, describes the nature of the attacks that have distorted understanding of the system, and makes a strong case that Social Security's benefits need to be substantially increased. He does not leave it at that, but suggests a workable way in which the expansion that he calls for can be achieved.

Everyone who is affected by Social Security should read this book. That means that virtually every American should do so. Reading it should help guard against the assaults on this essential program that continue, usually unrecognized. For example, although Social Security receives its funding from FICA taxes, its administrative expenses have to be approved by Congress. These funds do not affect the budget, but conservatives in Congress insist on squeezing appropriations, making it ever more difficult for the Social Security Administration to do its job. The more the funding is reduced, the fewer personnel it can employ to administer its programs, the more district offices it has to close, and the poorer the service it will be that it provides to Americans. Cuts to services can create unhappiness with Social Security, itself, and such unhappiness would play into the hands of those who wish to damage or eliminate this greatest of American programs.

This was amply described in a blog post from the Center on Budget and Policy Priorities. On June 9, 2016, Kathleen Romig, senior policy analyst for CBPP wrote:

Senate Bill Continues Eroding
Social Security Operating Funds

Kathleen Romig

June 9, 2016 at 3:30 PM

The 2017 funding bill for the departments of Labor, Health and Human Services, and Education that the Senate Appropriations Committee approved today would continue squeezing the Social Security Administration (SSA), which faces a record workload as the baby boomers age into their peak years for retirement and disability.

As our report explains, SSA's core operating budget shrank by 10 percent from 2010 to 2016, after adjusting for inflation. It would shrink another 1 percent under the Senate bill, after inflation.

The cuts have hampered the agency's ability to perform essential services like determining benefit eligibility promptly, paying benefits accurately and on time, and responding to the public's questions.

As a result, SSA's track record of exemplary customer service has suffered:

- A hiring freeze necessitated by budget cuts has harmed SSA phone service. Callers to SSA's 800 number average over 15 minutes on hold, and nearly 10 percent receive busy signals.

- SSA has had to close hundreds of field offices and mobile offices, and to reduce hours at remaining offices. As a result, a typical applicant must wait over 3 weeks for an appointment.

- When the number of applications for Social Security Disability Insurance rose dramatically in the Great

Recession, SSA lacked the resources to keep up with the spike in hearings for applicants appealing their rejections. The average wait for a hearing rose from 360 to 540 days between 2011 and 2016, and the hearings backlog grew to over 1 million, an all-time high.

- Lack of adequate staff forced SSA to delay critical behind-the-scenes work necessary to pay benefits accurately and on time, such as awarding widows' benefits when their spouses die and adjusting benefits for early retirees and disabled workers with earnings. Beneficiaries wait an average of 4 months for SSA to complete these tasks.

Nearly every American contacts SSA at some point—in person, on the phone, or through its expanding online services—and at the best and worst moments of their lives. They use SSA services when they have a baby, get married, or start a new job. They depend on SSA staff to help them when they face a life-altering disability, the death of a spouse or parent, or decisions about financing their retirement years. They expect excellent service and—importantly—they have paid for it. Social Security's administrative funding comes from workers' Social Security contributions, but only to the extent that Congress allows SSA to spend it.

Failing to invest in customer service is penny-wise and pound-foolish. As then-Social Security Commissioner Michael Astrue, appointed by President George W. Bush, told the Senate in 2012:

At some point, we will have to handle every claim that comes to us, every change of address, every direct deposit change, every workers' compensation change, every request for new or replacement Social Security cards. The longer it takes us to get to this work, the more it costs to do.

Policymakers should give SSA enough funding to give Americans the excellent Social Security service they have earned.[7]

The Entire System under Attack—

As important as Social Security is, however, it is only one part of America's political system, and the entire system is under concerted attack. As noted above, the attackers are enormously wealthy, well organized, and determined to shift all the levers of power away from elected officials into their own hands. If successful, this would lead directly to even greater increases in income disparity, and to massive escalation of poverty in the United States—and the efforts thus far have already achieved considerable success.

No one has documented this more fully than the superb investigative reporter, Jane Mayer, in her massive exposé, *Dark Money*. She begins by brilliantly introducing what she will be presenting. That will include her examination of what she aptly terms "the Kochtopus." She begins her narrative in 2009, discussing a gathering of the ultra wealthy in response to the panic they felt at the inauguration of Barack Obama. The new president had had the audacity to say critical things about them.

Mayer describes Charles Koch's reaction early in January to the Obama victory. He used "almost apocalyptic terms" in an "impassioned newsletter to his company's seventy-thousand employees." He said that Americans were facing "the greatest loss of liberty and prosperity since the 1930s," and warned of the dangers of increasing government spending. "Markets, not government," he argued were the only "engine for growth" (p. 6). Days later, Obama's inaugural address, she said, "lived up to his worst dreams," and were an attack on "the notion that markets work best when government regulates them least." Perhaps even more dangerous, in Koch's view was the presidential assertion that might have seemed simply to be common sense to most people, that "the nation cannot prosper long when it favors only the prosperous" (p. 7). Favoring only the prosperous, of course, is precisely what the Kochs and their co-conspirators had sought for so long.

Charles and David Koch, Mayer remarks, in any case would have had truly extraordinary influence simply because of their great wealth, "but for many years, they had magnified their reach further by joining forces with a small and intensely ideological group of like-minded political allies, many of whose personal fortunes were also unfathomably large." Fewer than 30 years previously, their views were so "far out on the political fringe" as to be described, perhaps laughingly, by "the conservative icon" of the time, William F. Buckley, Jr., "as Anarcho-Totalitarianism" (pp. 1–3).

Since that time, 1980, when Charles Koch had been the vice presidential candidate of the Libertarian Party garnering only 1% of the vote, the Kochs had been applying their engineering skills, buttressed by the pouring of "hundreds of millions of dollars into a stealthy effort to move their political views from the center to the fringe of American political life" (p. 3). Reagan's election had shifted that mainstream. Tellingly, it had brought openly into normal American politics a new, extremist, political rhetoric that not only became congenial to many voters, but was consistent with the goals of the Kochs. The candidacy of George Wallace in 1968 had paved the way for racist code words and "wink wink, nudge nudge" messages that had underlain Nixon's "Southern Strategy." That had blossomed under Reagan spreading far from the south, thereby creating a receptive climate for the efforts of the Kochs.

Mayer carefully studies the "networks of seemingly unconnected think tanks and academic programs," and the advocacy groups that the Kochs spawned "to make their argument in the national political debate. They hired lobbyists to push their interests in Congress and operatives to create synthetic grassroots groups to give their movement political momentum on the ground." Their efforts led, eventually, to a "private political machine that rivaled, and threatened to subsume, the Republican Party." Generally, this is done in such secrecy, "and presented as philanthropy," that it left "almost no money trail" (p. 3). The single-minded Kochs were not alone, and attracted other powerful allies. Many of these also came from families of the hyper-rich, including Richard Mellon Scaife (Mellon banking and Gulf Oil), Harry and Lynde Bradley (defense contractors), John M. Olin (chemicals and munitions), the Coors brewing family, and the DeVos family of Amway (Betsy DeVos, one should note, is currently Mr. Trump's secretary of education). By 2015, an operative boasted that the Kochs had created a "*fully integrated network*" [*sic*] (p. 4).

Incidentally, this led also to many similar efforts on a smaller scale, although looming enormous at state and local levels. In Missouri, for example, following the Koch example, Rex Sinquefield, a St. Louis multi-millionaire has endowed a "free-market" propaganda effort at the University of Missouri, the "Show-Me Institute." He has poured so much money directly into the state's politics (Missouri eliminated its limits on campaign contributions years ago) that many Republican legislators notoriously are reputed to ask, routinely, "have you run this by Rex?" when urged to support a given policy. Republicans, it should be noted, since the elections of 2000 have dominated the Missouri legislature, and hold veto-proof majorities in both legislative houses.

By the time Obama had taken office, the Kochs for years had been sponsoring "summits" of fellow billionaires, "no fewer than eighteen" of them (p. 9), that had come to deal in huge amounts of money to be used for influence, amounts that were entirely unprecedented. "Earlier businessmen had certainly spent outsized sums in hopes of manipulating American politics," Mayer writes, "but the numbers in the Koch seminars far outstripped those of the past." She quoted Dan Balz from *The Washington Post*, as saying that in 1972, when W. Clement Stone had given $2 million to the Nixon campaign (probably about $11 million in purchasing power today), there was so much "public outrage" that a movement emerged that resulted in the Watergate reforms in campaign finance. "In contrast, for the 2016 election, the political war chest accumulated by the Kochs and their small circle of friends, was projected to be $889 million, completely dwarfing the scale of money that was considered deeply corrupt during the Watergate days" (p. 8). Where was the outrage in 2016? It seemed mostly to be on the side of the Republicans who had convinced themselves that the simple fact of Obama's election itself demonstrated astronomical amounts of corruption from the Democrats.

"For years, American economists had tended to downplay the importance of economic inequality," Mayer notes correctly (p. 10). Their assumption was that markets would be self-correcting, and that the equality that is important, is equality of opportunity, not outcome. In view of the way in which they poured money into universities, boosting "free-market" solutions, one may be forgiven for suspecting that the lavish spending of the Kochs may have influenced scholars in their conclusions just as it did politicians (see chapter 4).

She quotes the late Milton Friedman that "a society that puts equality—in the sense of equality of outcome—ahead of freedom with end up with neither equality nor freedom. ... On the other hand, a society that puts freedom first will, as a happy by-product, end up with both greater freedom and greater equality" (p. 11). This clearly was a play upon the famous comment that Benjamin Franklin made (allegedly) that those who would give up essential liberty for temporary safety deserve neither liberty nor safety. In fact, even Franklin was referring to taxes, rather than to real freedom. Regardless, Friedman was spouting nonsense, based upon a strawman argument that no American in a powerful position has ever made—"equality of outcome!" Welcome Marx!—and was purely an expression of Friedman's prejudices, entirely unsupported by evidence.

The extent to which Friedman's understanding of "freedom" was warped is obvious in the extent to which he, and his "Chicago boys," colluded with the late and unlamented dictator in Chile, Augusto Pinochet. They gave every assistance to provide economic freedom to Chile's privileged elites, and Friedman was manifestly unconcerned about the harsh tyranny and torment that Pinochet imposed upon Chileans in general. To the detriment of the Chilean people, Pinochet could boast of full ideological support from that apostle of "freedom" (with apologies to Thomas Jefferson) Milton Friedman.

Republicans certainly could not be assumed to be unaware of the damage from such rigid ideology. Mayer quotes "Mike Lofgren, a Republican who spent thirty years observing how wealthy interests gamed the policymaking apparatus in Washington, where he was a staff member on the Senate Budget Committee," as decrying "the secession of the rich," who were disconnecting "themselves from the civic life of the nation and from any concern about its well-being except as a place to extract loot" (p. 11). She quotes Jacob Hacker and Paul Pierson (we will examine their arguments more fully below) to the effect that America had become a "'winner-take-all' country in which economic inequality perpetuated itself by pressing its political advantage." She remarked that if this were so, the Koch seminars "provided a group portrait of the winners' circle."

In contrast to the utopian scenario, the Kochs present as a result of their libertarian fantasy, the reality is far different. Koch Industries are known for their disregard of environmental safety, and for the dire effects that they have not only on their workers, but upon those who live near their installations.

Mayer discusses one tragic case representing a situation that is all too common. Despite warnings from four federal agencies that benzene is highly toxic, a powerful man, Donald Carlson, nicknamed "Bull," worked for Koch's Pine Bend Refinery in Rosemont, Minnesota, beginning in 1974, with no warnings of the hazards. "In particular, Carlson said, no one warned him about benzene"

(p. 121). "He cleaned out huge tanks that contained leaded gaso-line, scraping them down by hand. He took samples from storage tanks whose vapors escaped with such force they sometimes blew his helmet off." His wife recalled that he was "practically swim-ming in those tanks," but he didn't think twice about it. By 1995, he had become so progressively ill that he could no longer work. The company released him with 6 months' pay, and no workman's compensation. Although his blood cells had shown abnormalities in the legally-required blood tests, beginning in 1990, the com-pany had not informed him of the results until 1994, and had never referred him because of his abnormal results to medical specialists, as federal law required. "Charles Koch had disparaged government regulations as 'socialistic.' From his standpoint, the regulatory state that had grown out of the Progressive Era was an illegitimate encroachment on free enterprise and a roadblock to initiative and profitability" (p. 121). In 1997, Carlson died, at 53, of leukemia. His doctor "couldn't believe he was never put on workmen's comp" (p. 122). His widow, Doreen, conducted a long legal battle against the corporation, and finally won a settle-ment—minutes "before the case was to be heard by a judge." The settlement was contingent on a confidentiality agreement. After several years, the agreement expired, and she finally could speak out. She said it all was just "collateral damage." Regarding whether it was fair to blame the Kochs instead of lower-level executives, she said "Charles Koch owns the refinery." For them, it's simply money, and "they never have enough." They want anything that benefits them, and said, "I hear that they're backing a lot of people politically, and I bet it's all about getting rid of regulations." The regulations, though, she said, were for safety, not for making the workers rich. "It's so they don't die" (p. 122).

Charles, himself, wrote an article for *The Libertarian Review* in 1978. "We should *not* cave in the moment a regulator sets foot on our doorstep," he said. "Do not cooperate voluntarily; instead, resist wherever and to whatever extent you legally can. And do so in the name of *justice*" (p. 123). Whether his position reflects purely his economic self-interest or his basic beliefs is irrelevant. The effects are what matter. As Bull Carlson was dying, a "whistle blower" in Corpus Christi, Texas revealed that the company "was lying about illegal quantities of benzene that it was leaking into the air." Sally Barnes-Soliz, "a Koch Industries Environmental Technician," said "the refinery was just hemorrhaging benzene into the atmosphere." The company, however, attempted to cover it up (pp. 123–124). The company assigned her to a remote office with no duties and "no e-mail access." Eventually, she resigned, and in 1999 won a lawsuit against it for harassment. The settlement, of course, was sealed.

At about the same time, another Koch worker, Carnell Green, had been instructed to dump mercury on the ground from electric meters. After taking a class on hazardous materials, though, he reported to his supervisor that the material should be handled more carefully. Soon, he received a visit from a "Special Agent Moorman," who said he was from the FBI, and would send Green to jail if he did not retract his statements. Green later learned that "Special Agent Moorman" worked for Koch security in Wichita, Kansas, not for the FBI (pp. 125–126). So far as anyone knows, there has been no prosecution of "Special agent Moorman" for impersonating a federal agent.

Mayer says that of course "a few legal violations could be understood as misfortunate accidents." Koch Industries, however, was far different. It displayed a "pattern of pollution that was striking not just for its egregiousness but also for its willfulness" (p. 128). She mentions many other instances. Even so, she surely has only dealt with a relatively small number of the many outrages that the Kochs had committed.

Their effect on American politics is certainly reflected in the notoriety of the "Tea Party." The Kochs have denied any involvement, and "such denials helped shape the early narrative of the Tea Party movement as an amateur uprising by ordinary citizens" (p. 167).

The Tea Partiers' target has routinely been President Obama, and Tea Party outrage became a matter for headlines after an on-air rant on CNBC by a regular contributor, Rick Santelli, on February 19, 2009, just as Barack Obama was completing his very first month in office.

Regardless of his administration's mistakes, real and imagined, "it is hard," Mayer stresses, "to think of another president who had to face the kind of guerrilla warfare waged against him almost as soon as he took office. A small number of people with massive resources orchestrated, manipulated and exploited the economic unrest for their own purposes. They used tax-deductible donations to fund a movement to slash taxes on the rich and cut regulations on their own businesses" (p. 165). It is telling that the closest example was the other recent Democratic president, Bill Clinton.

Santelli "shrieked, 'This is America!' How many of you people want to pay your neighbor's mortgage?" and threatened to organize his own Chicago Tea Party after hearing that the president proposed an economic stimulus. Perhaps even worse, Obama had urged "help for the over-extended underclasses." Mayer notes just how ridiculous Santelli's comments were, and reminds us of Michael Grunwald's observation (in *The New New Deal*) that "the Boston Tea Party was a protest against an unelected leader who raised taxes, while Obama was an elected leader who had just cut them" (p. 166). To this day, it is a rare to find anyone, especially a Republican, who recognizes that Obama lowered taxes.

There were elements of spontaneity in the Tea Party's emergence, but the story that it emerged on its own from the grass roots is hardly the case, nor was it "a new strain" in American politics. Mayer points to similar venomous reactionary attacks on "every Democratic president since Franklin Roosevelt. Earlier business-funded right-wing movements, from the Liberty League to the John Birch Society [in which Charles Koch was prominent] to Scaife's Arkansas Project [aimed at destroying Bill Clinton's

presidency] all had cast Democratic presidents as traitors, usurp-
ers, and threats to the Constitution. The undeniable element of racial resentment that tinged many Tea Party rallies was also an old
and disgracefully enduring story in American politics" (p. 167).

It is equally wrong to accept the portrayal of the Tea Party as
nonpartisan. "As a *New York Times* poll later showed, over three
quarters of its supporters identified as Republican. The bulk of the
remainder felt the Republican Party was not Republican *enough*"
(*sic*) (p. 167). Without question, this purportedly "anti-elitist rebellion was funded, stirred, and organized by experienced political elites." Harvard scholars Theda Skocpol and Vanessa William-
son studied the Tea Party, and, as Mayer relates, they found that
the so-called mass uprising was "funded by corporate billionaires,
like the Koch brothers, led by over-the-hill former GOP kingpins
like Dick Armey [former Republican Majority Leader in the US
House], and ceaselessly promoted by millionaire media celebrities
like Glenn Beck and Sean Hannity" (pp. 167–168).

In fact, until relatively recently, the libertarian movement itself
was purely elitist. Economist Bruce Bartlett has said it had been
"all chiefs and no Indians." What the Kochs had attempted and
the Tea Party finally accomplished, he said, was that "everyone
sees that for the first time there are Indians out there" (quoted
p. 168). Previous attempts had had little success. Citizens for a
Sound Economy had attempted in 1991 to generate a reaction
against tax increases, this was in Raleigh, North Carolina, but
"the press corps nearly outnumbered the clutch of protesters in
Revolutionary War, Uncle Sam, and Santa Claus costumes." The
next year CSE tried to stage another Tea Party protests, this time
"secretly funded by tobacco companies to fight cigarette taxes,"
but it "canceled after its covert funding was exposed. By 2007,
Citizens for a Sound Economy had split up. The Kochs' new organization, Americans for Prosperity, tried to stage another Tea
Party protest against taxes, this time in Texas. It too was a dud"
(pp. 168–169).

Mayer makes plain the obstacles that President Obama faced from the very beginning. It was a "new form of permanent campaign," she writes, "waged not by politicians but by people whose wealth gave them the ability to fund their own field operations with which they could undermine the outcome of the election" (p. 169). As she notes, there was considerable attention to the funding from outside the actual campaigns that was associated with elections, but far less recognition of the rain of dollars in equal amounts falling upon "the way the country was governed" (169).

The billionaires concluded that they needed to spend even greater amounts, and so continuously, since those early efforts, they have generated huge numbers of position papers, "history lessons," op eds, and the like. These reflected the Koch conviction that government action causes trouble, including the Great Depression. They favored the policies of Warren Harding and Calvin Coolidge (who declared the "chief business of the American people is business"), and scorned Herbert Hoover and FDR, classifying them both as dangerous liberals (!). Right-wing scholars began to praise Coolidge (who, after all, allegedly was Ronald Reagan's favorite previous president), and condemn the New Deal as perpetuating the depression. That famous "liberal," Hoover, had made the same charge.

The Kochs praised the "Robber Barons" as great Americans, and mobilized the "Kochtopus, the sprawling network of some thirty-four public policy and political organizations" that Koch money had created. Their think tanks—the Cato Institute, the Heritage Foundation, and the Hoover Institution at Stanford University—produced a flood of propaganda attacking President Obama's stimulus plan, much of which more objective scholars soon discredited. Some of the material was simply false. The Mercatus Center, a Koch-funded unit at George Mason University, released a study purporting to show that the administration directed stimulus funds disproportionately to Democratic districts. "Eventually, the author was forced to correct the report, but not before Rush Limbaugh, citing the paper, had labeled Obama's program a 'slush fund' and Fox News and other conservative outlets had echoed the sentiment" (p. 171). These and other "paid advocates," formed what many observers, including Mayer, have described as an echo chamber. "Phil Kerpen, the vice president for policy at Americans for Prosperity, was a contributor to the Fox News web site. Another officer at Americans for Prosperity, Walter Williams, the John M. Olin Distinguished Professor of Economics at George Mason University, was a frequent guest host on Limbaugh's radio show, which claimed to have an audience of twenty million listeners" (p. 171).

Immediately after Obama's electoral victory in 2008, the new House minority whip, Eric Cantor of Virginia, met with a group of House allies and forged themselves into the "Young Guns." They saw their duty as simply to obstruct Obama, arguing that they needed to oppose virtually anything the new president proposed "in order to deny him a single bipartisan victory." Pete Sessions, one of the group, called for adopting the strategy of Afghanistan's Taliban. Regardless of the economic meltdown, he argued, they had not been elected to govern. That was the majority's job. The insurgents had only one responsibility: to become the majority (p. 172). They were convinced that the only reason the Republicans lost was because they were not conservative enough.

For his part, Obama "continued to seek bipartisan support. His experience with what Hillary Clinton labeled the 'vast right-wing conspiracy' was limited" (p. 174). Those who had more such experience, were dismayed that he kept assuming that the Republicans would work in good faith, and so he kept affording them the opportunity to be like Lucy, in the comic strip "Peanuts," who continually reassured Charlie Brown that this time would be different; that she would cooperate, and hold the football for him to kick. Invariably, she yanked it away, and he fell flat on his back. Symbolically, Republicans did the same to President Obama. Reporters had ridiculed Clinton in the 1990s when she made the conspiracy comment, but she was completely accurate, as should now be painfully obvious to any observer.

As the Republican-dominated Congress has shifted so far to the right, the influence of the Kochs and their allies has become obvious. For much of their careers, the Kochs have shunned publicity, but their influence now is so pervasive that it cannot be ignored. They have begun to "portray themselves as disinterested do-gooders and misunderstood social liberals who championed bipartisan issues such as criminal justice reform" (p. 272).

Certainly, the Kochs have contributed substantially to medical research and to the arts, and undoubtedly, there is an urgent need for criminal justice reform. The Koch interest in the topic, though, turns primarily on a desire to reduce the power of federal prosecutors to hold them and their industries to account for such violations as environmental damage. "In *Plutocrats: The Rise of the New Global Super Rich and the Fall of Everyone Else*, the journalist Chrystia Freeland describes how those with massive financial resources almost universally use them to secure policies beneficial to their interests, often at the expense of the less well-off. In the United States, a number of studies have shown that in recent years this tendency has distorted politics in very specific ways" (pp. 272–273).

Much of that distortion has come, by design, at the state level. States are where much of the basic legal structure exists, and where the great promise of gerrymandering and overt voter suppression has borne fruit for the far right. One of the major influences at the state level has been ALEC (the American Legislative Exchange Council), a brainchild of Paul Weyrich, one of the earliest in the modern movement of right-wing extremists. It defines itself as nonprofit, and thus receives tax exemption. One of its most effective activities has been to write hundreds of draft bills incorporating policies of the far right and sending them to state legislatures where legislators introduce them as their own (see pp. 246–247).

The sudden political disaster in North Carolina, historically the most progressive state in the south, is a case study in the possibilities of the importance of the states, and their vulnerabilities to the politics of destruction. "From the Civil War on through the civil rights movement, states' rights had been a conservative rallying cry, particularly in the South. Historically, it had often been bound up in racial animosities" (p. 345). We now see a proliferation of firearms, of "stand your ground" laws (laws that seemingly benefit only armed aggressors, never the unarmed Trayvon Martins who are assassinated), and other irrationalities. We see also resistance (because expansion would be part of "Obamacare") in Republican states to expansion of Medicaid that would greatly benefit the people, bring more money into hard pressed states, and be paid for almost entirely by the national government.

Mayer quotes "Thomas A. Roe, an anti-union construction magnate from Greenville, South Carolina," as reportedly having said "to a fellow trustee at the Heritage Foundation during the 1980s, 'You capture the Soviet Union—I'm going to capture the states'" (p. 345). In 1992, he founded the State Policy Network, which Mayer describes as "a national coalition of conservative think tanks turning out cookie-cutter-like policy papers, including at least one hub in every state" (p. 345). In 2009, it spun off its own "investigative news" service that partnered with a new "Franklin Center for Government and Public Integrity," and drew much of the "news" items that it fed to state and local outlets from the State Policy Network and the legislative proposals from ALEC. The Franklin Center quickly had centers in "some forty states" (p. 347).

The results are plain, not only in North Carolina, but in state after state. Louisiana and Kansas are two of the most notorious: basket cases, because of the policies of the True Believers, former Louisiana Governor Bobby Jindal, and current Kansas Governor Sam Brownback.

Little Kansas—containing the heart of Wichita-based Koch empire—recently again received unwelcome front page publicity in the *New York Times* (not to mention in the *Kansas City* Star) because of the stubborn insistence by Governor Brownback that his draconian policies of slashing taxes, especially on business, are working. This, as public schools are considering closing, industries are shunning the state, potholes are jarring more and more motorists, state agencies find it increasingly difficult to do their jobs, the Legislature has removed all restrictions on the carrying of firearms, the same legislature has empowered its power-hungry secretary of state, Kris Kobach, with police powers so that he can chase his imagined hordes of unqualified voters (who, apparently, re-elected him and Brownback to office in spite of the two officials' massive failures), and so forth. The Kansas legislature has even gone so far as to attempt to de-fund the state's judiciary because its rulings are aimed at holding the legislature to the state's constitution.

Mitch McConnell, the Republican Majority Leader of the U.S. Senate, spoke at the Kochs' donor summit in June 2015. He "thanked 'Charles and David' and added," reports Mayer, "I don't know where we would be without you" (p. 371). Indeed.

Under the leadership of the far right, there is no hope in the current Congress for "addressing global warming," for dealing with economic inequality, for raising taxes on the very rich or closing loopholes designed to benefit them, and only them, or for "funding basic services like the repair of America's crumbling infrastructure." Nor would there be any prospect for Congress to combat the irrational assertion that, with regard to Social Security, "to save the program it needed to be shrunk" (p. 374).

Obama's re-election victory in 2012 seemed to be a defeat for the Kochs and their brethren. As has been made clear, though, their power at the deepest of levels was unimpaired. Obamacare had survived, "and polls showed that it was growing in popularity," but its reputation, and Obama's, was greatly damaged, "even though the country's health-care costs and medical coverage, like the economy as a whole, were far better off than before he took office Unemployment was down, and incomes and markets were up. Yet faith in government reached new lows" (p. 374).

"During the 1970s, a handful of the nation's wealthiest corporate captains felt overtaxed and overregulated and decided to fight back." They were "disenchanted with modern America." Merely winning elections was not what they wanted, "they wanted to change how Americans thought. Their ambitions were grandiose—to 'save' America as they saw it at every level, by turning the clock back to the Gilded Age." It is not too much to say, as Mayer does (quoting Brian Doherty) that Charles Koch "wanted to pull government out by the root" (p. 375).

They have masked themselves as public spirited, but what they want is power. One of their Koch Industries managers, Phil Dubose, "spent twenty-six years working for the Kochs before testifying against them in court," he had no doubt, and pulled no punches. They intended, he said, to get their own way, and they were determined to control all three branches of government. "They call themselves libertarians," Mayer quotes him. "For a lack of a better word, what it means is that if you're big enough to get away with it, you can get away with it. No government. If it's good for their business, they think it's good for America." As for the little people, he said, "They'd get gobbled up" (p. 377).

Jane Mayer is a splendid investigative reporter. She is a writer of courage, and has withstood efforts to silence her. The result is a thorough study that is an excellent analysis of today's American politics. What she has done is extremely important. It is no exaggeration to say that her book is a call to arms, if arms can be defined as the votes of an enlightened public that determines to exercise its right to cast them.

MAX J. SKIDMORE

Calling Attention to the Real History of America—

Jacob Hacker and Paul Pierson come together for the third time to continue their keen insights into the nature of American politics and into many of the troubles that plague the country: primarily, to explain how the political system veered so suddenly, and so sharply, to the right, tilted its policies ever more greatly to favor the very wealthy at the expense of everyone else, and in this current volume to reveal how right-wing propaganda has managed to falsify the role of government in American political history. It is little wonder that Bill Moyers has provided a blurb describing them as "the Sherlock Holmes and Dr. Watson of political science," and says, "they're marvelous." It is in no way to diminish their work to say that much of its value comes from their keen ability to recognize relevant facts and work with them, rather than in discovering surprising things that no one has known before. Hacker and Pierson have perfected the ability to identify things that all well-informed people should in fact already know, but for whatever reason, or reasons, very few of them do. In presenting such facts and describing why it is that they no longer command attention—even when they should be clear and obvious—team Hacker and Pierson have produced truly brilliant work. They deal with the quite serious substance that concerned the late humorist Will Rogers when he (allegedly) said: "it ain't what people don't know that's so dangerous—it's what people *know*, that *just ain't so!*"

American Amnesia follows their two previous efforts, *Winner-Take-All Politics: How Washington Made the Rich Richer—And Turned Its Back on the Middle Class*, and the thoughtful *Off Center: The Republican Revolution and the Erosion of American Democracy*. The subtitle here, *How the War on Government Led Us to Forget What Made America Prosper*, follows those of its predecessors in superbly capturing the substance of the books to which they are attached.

Casting the inside-the-Beltway dedication to tact (at least as it pertains to conservatives) aside, Hacker and Pierson begin by boldly asserting what they call an "uncomfortable truth." To be sure, it is uncomfortable, to Americans anyway, but it also is undeniable to anyone who functions in the real, as opposed to the fanciful, world: "It takes government—a lot of government—for advanced societies to flourish" (1). The humorist, Stephen Colbert in his previous incarnation put it succinctly, and with dead-on-the bullseye accuracy, when he said: "reality has a well-known liberal bias." Regardless of how fervently the Tea Party adherents and their billionaire angels hold to the notion that the Founders created the Constitution to weaken the national government, the Founding generation knew better.

Even when Jefferson in the Declaration of Independence asserted the ringing cry of "certain inalienable rights," he followed with, as Hacker and Pierson put it, the "clear-eyed recognition that 'to secure these rights, governments are instituted among men'—fifty-five notables gathered in Philadelphia because they had become convinced that the *absence of effective public authority was a mortal threat to the fledgling nation*" [italics added]. As the Rick Perrys speak favorably of secession, the Cliven Bundys along with sons and followers sit in jail because they flout the law, and a coven of billionaires works to transfer power from the public into their own hands the forgotten fact is that the Founders came together to bring forth a Constitution that would provide a strong central government, not render it impotent. "Perhaps the most influential of them all, James Madison, put the point bluntly in arguing against those at the Virginia ratifying convention who worried that the Constitution would create too strong a national government: 'There never was a government without force. What is the meaning of government? An institution to make people do their duty,'" but, they concede, Americans traditionally have not been good at acknowledging "government's necessary role," and they are worse at it now. And, we are suffering accordingly (p. 1).

Hacker and Pierson argue that markets and government require *"constructive and mutually beneficial tension (sic)* between markets and government rather than the jealous rivalry that so many misperceive—and, in this misperception, help foster." They make it clear that government sometimes overreaches, but that is far from the problem now. The trouble America faces is that it has "too little effective government, not too much" (pp. 2–3). They go into detail explaining why it is that markets need government to function. Some of their key points are that collective goods are essential that markets cannot provide, such as courts, basic infrastructure, education, and basic scientific research. There are also "spillover costs" that markets cannot handle, such as those from pollution (Koch brothers, take notice). Both consumers and investors need regulation to provide protection against "corporate predation (collusion, fraud, harm)" and from individuals' own myopic behavior, such as "smoking, failing to save, underestimating economic risks." Moreover, some insurance protections are necessary, as are mechanisms to lower risk from financial crises. They quote Adam Smith as recognizing that taxation must exist, and that regulation can be helpful so long as it does not benefit one commercial interest over another. It is always just and equitable, Smith said, to regulate in favor "of the workmen." This is far from the notion of Smith as an opponent of effective governance (pp. 4–5).

As I put it in the title of a recent article, "Anti-Government Is Not the Solution to Our Problem; Anti-Government IS the Problem." The article dealt with the need for a strong presidency in dealing with disasters, natural and otherwise, but the point remains.[8]

Hacker and Pierson quite correctly speak of human solutions to human problems. The mixed economy, which includes strong elements both of private markets and of government activity, is an example. "Private capitalism and public coercion each predated modern prosperity." Moreover, what libertarians and Tea Partiers seem to assume is a fact of nature, the market itself—and even the very notion of property itself—is socially constructed. Private property is not God given; it is what a given society, through its government, determines it is. Note, for example, that under some circumstances and in some places, when buying a home, the buyer does not buy the land, and must continue to pay "ground rent." In some areas, New Mexico, for example, a property "owner" may not have title to the minerals underneath the ground. Some things that might appear obvious elsewhere, surely would seem less so in these jurisdictions.

When a man walks across your lawn, he presumably is trespassing. If he were to fly over it at 30,000 feet, he certainly is not (despite the fulmination of the late U.S. Senator John Marshall Butler in the 1950s that if the new Soviet satellite were to fly over the United States, we would shoot the vile intruder down!). If the man were to send a drone, or even to fly an ultralight aircraft, over your lawn at 30 feet, would he be trespassing? What about 100 feet? Perhaps 1,000 feet? At what point above the ground does a right of property cease to exist? The question is, who determines. Certainly, it is the government in the form of law that makes the determination. Common sense understanding may and no doubt should have influence on the characteristics of the law, but such understandings can and do vary among societies and cultures. Nature does not dictate the extent of property "rights," nor does it create any such rights.

In today's legal and cultural struggles, "the most active combatants are not simply taking issue with recent departures from their preferred policies. They are taking issue with the entire edifice of modern public authority." Rather than thinking things went wrong in the 1970s, some "think things went wrong even earlier than that. They conjure up a mythical vision of the Constitution's authors as free-market fundamentalists and of the country's early economic rise as a triumph of laissez-faire. They downplay the depredations of the industrial economy that first prompted social reform and celebrate as geniuses and giants the men whom previous generations called 'robber barons.'" They cast the blame on a Democratic president, but for many of them it is not FDR; rather it is Woodrow Wilson "the southern-born governor of New Jersey who became president of the United States." The authors note that those on the left now criticize Wilson for the "intensely racist views he brought to the White House" (9), but (of course) this is not the substance of the criticisms from the right.

From the right, there is a "virulent, obsessive hatred" that goes beyond "bordering on hysteria" as Hacker and Pierson remark, quoting historian David Greenberg. The none-too-thoughtful Jonah Goldberg calls Wilson the first "fascist dictator." The less-than-stable Glenn Beck has said, "Oh how I hate that guy," and puts Wilson at the apex of history's "Ten Top Bastards," ahead of everyone, including "Hitler and Pol Pot." What was Wilson's crime? He built the mixed economy with such mechanisms as legislation creating the Federal Reserve System and anti-trust programs (p. 10). However much these mechanisms have improved the economy and made it function far better than previously, to the right they represent the evils of "statism." They seem to define any society that has a functioning government as "statist," to be condemned. Perhaps most heretical of all, they condemn Wilson for concluding that "the Constitution was not meant to hold the government back to the time of horses and wagons." Rather, he saw the Constitution and the economy as growing, and adapting together. Opponents such as the often sought after George Will (who demonstrates that the pompous can be mistaken for the profound) work themselves into an outraged fury at such notions (p. 11).

As for Wilson having "ruined the twentieth century," as many of the more fervent voices from the right, including Will, allege, of course that century included some horrible things, and "all centuries have their ups and downs." Despite its low points, though, Hacker and Pierson remind us that the twentieth "was an extraordinary one for the United States and the larger community of emerging affluent democracies." George Will may think Wilson ruined the century, but that century "brought greater increases in human prosperity—measured not just by income but also by life expectancy and education and much else—than the entirety of prior human history" (pp. 12–13).

Despite all the posturing on the right, the Philadelphia Convention did not emerge to produce a system incorporating gridlock. The Convention took place because the members perceived the Articles of Confederation as disastrous. Why was that? Because the Articles did not create a strong national government. The Convention sought strength, not weakness, at the center. Madison lost out, but had even attempted to provide the national government with the power to veto acts and laws of states.

Now, however, the right that has brought "the demonization of Woodrow Wilson," has morphed "Madison into some sort of pro-tolibertarian." That is, say Hacker and Pierson, the very "manifestation of American amnesia. The position embraced by George Will and other self-proclaimed 'constitutional conservatives' isn't the position of James Madison. It's the position of those who opposed creating the Constitution in the first place" (p. 12).

Perhaps that explains the inconsistencies of so many conservatives today. Although they purport to be Constitution worshippers, in reality they seek to make dramatic changes in the document that they pretend to revere.* The changes they seek are not limited to repealing amendments they dislike, such as the Fourteenth that provides birthright citizenship, the Sixteenth that authorizes the hated income tax, and even the Seventeenth that provides that the citizens of a state will elect that state's U.S. senators, instead of giving the selection to the state's legislature. When state legislators choose U.S. senators, those senators were more than "typically well-insulated from voters." As journalist William Allen White put it, note Hacker and Pierson, the Senate then constituted "a

---

* Max J. Skidmore, "The Constitution: We Love it; It's Perfect; Let's Change it!" *Huffington Post* (January 23 2015).

'millionaires' club where a member 'represented something more than a state, more even than a region He represents principalities and powers in businesses. One Senator ... represents the Union Pacific Railway System; another the New York Central; still another the insurance interests of New York and New Jersey'" (p. 92). Thus, as bizarre as it may seem for presumably "populist" conservatives to want to deny to voters the power to choose their U.S. senators, the reason is that they recognize that they, and business interests, would have an even easier time in selecting (and they hope) in controlling senators. Conservative desire for constitutional change extends to revisions in the original document. For example, many would change lifetime appointments for federal judges.

Regardless of conservative economists' arguments that rolling back regulation increases competition, the reality today is far different. Corporate influence currently has increased. "The main vehicle of rent delivery isn't overregulation that limits competition. Instead, it's indirect gifts to companies or economic sectors that seem on the surface to be operating as 'free' markets. Most blatantly, huge public resources in land, mineral, and grazing rights (and in modern times bandwidth) have been transferred at prices way below market value" (p. 93).

Mitt Romney's corporate world is considerably different from that of his father, George Romney. Even more fundamentally, it is far more "financialized." When George Romney headed American Motors companies tended to be bound to their communities, and often felt—and accepted—obligations to those communities and to their workers. Now, "the financial rewards at the top, both on Wall Street and in executive suites, generate enormous fortunes," so much so that "these concentrated resources threaten to swamp democratic government." Today, the situation has changed drastically. Any "incentive for CEOs to consider other stakeholders" is virtually gone. In George Romney's time, "government and organized labor, the two major sources of 'countervaiing power' (to use economist John Kenneth Galbraith's famous phrase), once encouraged business leaders to negotiate and seek mutually beneficial compromises. Now unions are almost gone from the private sector and government leaders are much less willing to use public authority to create beneficial constraint" (pp. 16–17).

The Republican Party has changed similarly. The future of the party turned out not to be that of George Romney, but rather of Barry Goldwater. "Romney's son would inherit the kind of party that the elder Romney had warned about. The issue that had split George Romney and Barry Goldwater—civil rights—soon split the Democratic Party and reinvigorated Republicans in the South. Even more fateful for George Romney's economic agenda, Goldwater's libertarianism became the lodestar for an economic philosophy centered on tax cuts, deregulation, and hostility toward both government and organized labor" (pp. 16–17).

Hacker and Pierson do not shy away from identifying the source of much that has gone wrong in American politics. They wisely lay the blame at the doorstep of Ronald Reagan, reminding us that it was Reagan who pointed the way to the future for the party. He had accused Republican moderates of "betrayal," and had sided with Goldwater over Romney and his allies. Reagan rejected Romney's vision of "industrial partnership and political compromise, marking out a rightward path along which his party continues to march" (17). However, much today's Republicans cast an aura of sainthood over Reagan, he laid the foundation for the progressively greater extremism of his Republican successors, and made it possible for the Gingrichs, DeLays, Bushs, Cheneys, McConnells, and their allies to poison today's political well.

The introductory portion of *American Amnesia* deftly sets the scene for the more detailed presentation of the bulk of the book. Populations crossed a "Great Divide," when governments cleaned up milk and water. "Thomas Jefferson lost five of the six children he had with his wife, Martha, who died after giving birth to the last. Lincoln saw two of his four sons die in childhood; a third died at age eighteen." Rutherford Hayes lost six of his children before reaching 2 years of age (p. 47). "By the end of the twentieth century, however, infant mortality in the United States was around 7 in 1,000, or 0.7 percent." That is higher than it should be, and is worse than in "peer nations," but nevertheless "it is more than 90 percent lower than a century earlier" (p. 48). There also were great advances in health because of medicines, especially antibiotics and vaccines. "In fact, both were largely products of the combined energy of scientists—usually publicly funded—and government agencies. More important, neither would have had the positive effects they did if not for extensive public action and substantial government constraints on individual freedom" (p. 51).

The longevity explosion in advanced societies, as Hacker and Pierson call it, also required something more than improved medical science and sanitation. The key was "expanded government efforts to broaden the quality of and access to medical care." These were "public investments in the infrastructure of care and in medical research and education, the creation of programs of national health insurance, and reforms designed to slow the increase of costs while safeguarding health" (p. 54). These improvements were anything but a "natural market development" (p. 55). They came because of refusal to rely on the market, and a recognition that market forces cannot generate needed improvements. The United States has progressed along with other advanced societies, but it has tended to lag behind their accomplishments, and because of this has paid the price—literally, because this country pays far more for much less health protection than its peers do.

As societies advance, they of course take on different characteristics, and many of those have to do with market failure. As Hacker and Pierson put it, "metaphors of the frontier and rugged individuals aside, the reality is that we continue to become ever more interconnected." They proceed to assert that "the richer we get, the more government we need" (p. 75), and they provide support for the assertion. Additionally, "all rich states are welfare states," they say, and they support this as well (p. 87). As wedded as Americans often are to Jeffersonian rhetoric, observers have noted through the years that they tend to welcome Hamiltonian practices.

As an aside, it may be appropriate here to mention Theodore Roosevelt. In his autobiography, he said that he admired Hamilton, yet "differed from Alexander Hamilton" in being a stout adherent of "Abraham Lincoln's views wherever the rights of the people are concerned."[9] That is quite a model for Republicans. One can hope that they regain their heritage, but all current indications are that this cannot happen.

For now, under the sway of the Kochtopus, it is tempting to give in to despair. A bit of perspective, however, may help. Although the situation is far worse than before, it is not unique. As Franklin Roosevelt strained to lift the United States out of the morass of the Great Depression, the business community rebelled, and "reverted to its antigovernment traditions, in 1935, business conservatives staged something akin to a coup at the Chamber of Commerce, until then the bastion of moderation within the corporate community. The year before, the fiercely antigovernment du Pont brothers (Pierre, Irenee, and Lammot) had used the proceeds of their vast trust to bankroll the archconservative American Liberty League, which portrayed the New Deal as an enemy of freedom. The league made defense of the Constitution as its rallying cry but the alternative names it considered—the Association Asserting the Rights of Property, the National Property League, and the American Federation of Business—indicated its main priorities" (pp. 131–132).

The following should sound familiar to anyone familiar with today's politics. "In addition to the du Ponts, the Liberty League's leadership included Alfred P. Sloan, president of General Motors; Edward F. Hutton, the founder of General Foods; and J. Howard Pew, president of Sun Oil The league's financial and organizational resources soon rivaled those of the Republican Party, and rhetorical fireworks between corporate America and the New Dealers intensified. Liberty League pamphlets attacked New Deal initiatives as fascist socialism and un-American, and compared FDR to Hitler, Mussolini, and Stalin." FDR responded vigorously, counterattacking before an enormous crowd in Philadelphia, calling the reactionaries "economic royalists." He said they took money from others, and used it to impose "a new industrial dictatorship." Later, "he told a raucous crowd at Madison Square Garden that 'organized money' was 'unanimous in their hate for me—and I welcome their hatred'" (pp. 131–132).

As Hacker and Pierson put it, "Republicans got the first of many political lessons when their 1936 presidential nominee, Alf Landon, called for repeal of Social Security, calling it a 'cruel hoax': 'unjust, unworkable, stupidly drafted, and wastefully financed.' Crushed by FDR ... Landon was the last GOP nominee for almost seventy years to challenge Social Security directly" (p. 148). They point out that no Republican candidate has ever received fewer electoral votes than Landon. He received eight, tying with Taft in 1912, who ran not only behind the winning Woodrow Wilson, but also the third-party Theodore Roosevelt.

In 1964, the Republican nominee Barry Goldwater lost to Lyndon B. Johnson, who was the only presidential candidate to reach 61% of the popular vote (only three other presidents had ever reached 60%: FDR in 1936, Nixon in 1972, and Harding in 1920). After each of these great losses, there were speculations that the Party might ultimately go the way of the Whigs.

Republicans struggled, however, and fought their way back to win the presidency in 1952 with Dwight Eisenhower, and briefly to claim congressional majorities as well. Eisenhower faced Democratic majorities in both congressional houses for his last 6 years as president, but he had a successful presidency, characterized by acceptance of the basic outlines of FDR's New Deal.

The Republican resurgence after the Goldwater fiasco was much more rapid. They won the presidency with Richard Nixon in the election of 1968, and won once again with Nixon's landslide re-election in 1972, only to have Nixon forced from office because of manifest misconduct. His administration had stunning successes, though, as well as the depths of enormous failure.

Despite Nixon's successes, the failed part of his administration—influenced by the racial politics of the populist demagogue, George Wallace, in his own third-party presidential candidacy as Nixon won in 1968—established the conditions that grew during the presidencies of the Reagan years and those of the first Bush. With the emergence of the skilled and energetic activism of Newt Gingrich and Tom DeLay, the atmosphere was such that the growing themes blossomed into full-fledged anti-government, anti-tax, anti-science, highly ideological approaches conditioned by the party's alliance with the most conservative evangelical fundamentalists, all held together in spite of their differing theologies by fervent anti-abortion obsession and a desire to dominate America politically and socially. The growing extremism brought a hysterical impeachment of one Democratic president, Bill Clinton, and an even more hysterical reaction to the next Democratic president, Barack Obama, whom his opponents—consumed by their own fears and hatreds—had come to believe was the personification of evil, to be resisted in every instance, regardless of what he proposed. That the party seems to have forgotten its success when functioning within the mainstream of American politics seems apparent in the reaction to Obama's Affordable Care Act, which contains more than echoes of the 1936 Landon reaction to FDR's Social Security Act.

After Obama took office, there was a brief period when the business community "by all accounts," received the new "president's remarks with enthusiasm." Very shortly, however, "it was business leaders and their Republican allies carrying the pitchforks. Over the course of 2009 and 2010, business lobbies spent never-before-seen amounts to defeat or defang the Obama agenda, with Wall Street, the energy industry, and business groups leading the charge. Under its combative head, Tom Donohue, the US Chamber of Commerce launched the largest legislative campaign in its history." Business leaders decried Obama's "betrayal," they said he had "vilified" and "demonized" them (p. 156). They were stung by comments that were far milder than those FDR had flung at their predecessors. *Forbes* magazine called Obama "the most anti-business president in a generation, perhaps in American history." The multi-billionaire Stephen Schwarzman "railed that the president had declared 'war' by seeking to close a notorious tax loophole allowing some of the nation's wealthiest financiers to pay just 15 percent federal taxes on much of their incomes" (p. 157).

The president's opponents had worked themselves into a frenzy, and were convinced that he "had embarked on an unprecedented left-wing campaign. Yet," note Hacker and Pierson, "the president's agenda, though ambitious, was hardly the leftist project caricatured by his critics," and most of his proposals "sidestepped more liberal alternatives." The reaction said more about how the business community had changed than it did about Obama (pp. 158–159). It also said more about how the Republican Party had changed.

There is no doubt that the reaction to Obama reflected racist undertones, some of them overt. This is not, however, the entire story. "Clinton felt the vice tightening from the first days of his presidency" (p. 163). The far right had come to perceive any Democratic president as illegitimate, and acted accordingly. When Obama proposed a program that would sharply reduce the number of Americans who had no access to healthcare, he reached out consistently to Republicans, and consistently received rebuffs. The program as passed, nevertheless, was built almost entirely on Republican ideas, but, as Hacker and Pierson comment, "yesterday's Great Republican Idea is today's socialist plot" (p. 242).

American Amnesia is a thoughtful, well-written, and powerful indictment of the way in which American politics now fails to function, and how that political failure was deliberately contrived. The engineers of the destruction—the authors lay the blame most strongly at the doorsteps of Newt Gingrich and Mitch McConnell (p. 260)—proceed to halt government progress regardless of the consequences for the country. They operate "by stirring up (and making up) scandals" (p. 308), misrepresenting American history, describing existing government programs falsely, and attempting not merely to defeat their opponents politically, but to destroy them.

There is much more in this fine book. It covers many subjects, and presents great detail. A section title late in the volume, though, suffices to sum up its well-documented findings clearly: "The Government that Governs Least ... Governs Pretty Badly" (p. 320).

It's Not Nice to Lie—

The discussion above, including the reviews of the three books already considered, brings us to *Lies, Incorporated*. The title is intemperate. The opening sentence (in the Preface, itself titled "Liar") is even more so. "Richard Berman is a liar," it begins with no hesitation (p. xi). The authors are Ari Rabin-Havt and Media Matters. Rabin-Havt hosts *The Agenda*, a weekly show on satellite radio. He previously was with Media Matters for America as executive vice president, and has served as adviser to former Vice President Al Gore, and to the Democratic leader of the U.S. Senate, Harry Reid. Media Matters is a progressive website that describes itself as monitoring conservative misinformation wherever it appears in American news media. It is unabashedly a pro-Hillary Clinton publication. Whatever allowances one may wish to make because of all this, the "lies" that *Lies, Incorporated* identifies and discusses, by any objective measure are indeed lies.

However intemperate the opening sentence is, the discussion justifies it immediately. It even suggests that Berman, himself, might agree with the characterization. Perhaps he would; and go so far as to take pride in it.

The book declares that he "earns his living profiting from the invention and trafficking of lies. The fast-food industry, tobacco companies, and high-fructose corn syrup producers have all called upon him to do what few others would: shamelessly spread falsehoods, smear the reputations of well-regarded nonprofit groups, and purchase phony research." Industries that are besieged summon him when they decide as a last resort that they must engage in the "nastiest of PR campaigns." Berman "relishes the title of 'Dr. Evil,' [and] is not just an operator for sale to the highest bidder. He is the purest representation of a growing force in American politics that creates and disseminates lies designed to disrupt the public policy process for monetary and ideological gain" (p. xi). It is revealing, as well as astonishing, to look behind many of the most misleading advertising campaigns, and discover the same names over and over.

Many observers have noted that the truth often appears to be irrelevant in modern American politics. This book gives some explanations as to how this has come about. Lewis Powell, later to be an associate justice of the U.S. Supreme Court, in 1971 sent a memo to Eugene Sydnor, who chaired the U.S. Chamber of Commerce's "Education Committee." Powell proposed a national effort to influence public opinion in favor of business, and complained that the business community had too little influence on public policy (p. 13). Whatever the influence of Powell's memorandum—conspiracy theories, of course, proliferate, and may exaggerate the memorandum's significance—there is no question that the amount of business lobbying since that time has mushroomed. It now constitutes far more than the combined amounts spent by others (p. 14). Additionally, "think tanks" have proliferated. "Most of these institutions do not consist of scholars developing solutions unmoored to ideology or funding. Instead, many are simply part of an ideological arsenal" (p. 16).

Moreover, things are not always as them seem. "In March 2015, a group called American Commitment boasted it sent 1.6 million messages asking Congress to take action to overturn the Federal Communication Commission's net neutrality ruling." Immediately, there were charges that many of the "messages" were false. "Some members of Congress who responded to these communications received replies claiming the constituent in question 'had never signed up to send emails criticizing net neutrality'" (p. 18). Even "good" organizations have been known to trade their support on matters outside their concerns in return for corporate contributions" (p. 19).

The forces at work, it seems, may be far more important and coordinated than even the authors recognized. The efforts by American billionaires and other powerful interests in the country would have been powerful (and sinister) enough, but they are not the only forces at work. Numerous news reports in Autumn of 2017 indicate that there are numerous and well-documented efforts directed by the Russian government aimed at destabilizing the American political system, encouraging secessionist sentiments (both here and in other countries), sabotaging Hillary Clinton's presidential campaign, and otherwise sowing and encouraging discord—even to the extent of disunion—in the United States.

Certainly, as *Lies Incorporated* puts it, we live in a "world of post-truth politics." This has come about because a political culture has developed that accepts "ideological victory, not progress," as the ultimate goal (p. 21).

Lies, Incorporated proceeds to present a number of chapters, each devoted to a monstrous lie perpetuated by political interest groups motivated by personal gain—that is, by greed. The first of these, appropriately, is tobacco, which it defies as "the birth of Lies, Incorporated" (chapter 1). This is less of an issue today than it was previously because the dangers of tobacco are so overwhelming as finally to have been widely accepted, and restrictions on smoking widely adopted. The harrowing truth, though, is that the industry worked diligently to obscure the issues, and cast doubt upon the clear scientific findings demonstrating tobacco's dangers—dangers about which tobacco executives themselves were under no illusions. The industry succeeded for years in creating public doubt about the ravages of tobacco use so that it could maintain sales, and profits.

"Tobacco's Sequel" follows, and that is climate change. *Lies, Incorporated* credits *Merchants of* Doubt, by Naomi Oreskes and Erik Conway, for having presented much of the evidence against industry campaigns against science regarding tobacco and global warming. In 1998, the American Petroleum Institute, the industry lobbying group, developed a plan to defeat the proposed Kyoto treaty. The strategy was to challenge the science that demonstrated human causes for the undeniable warming of the planet. Some respected scientists who were elderly Cold Warriors, and apparently fearful that governments sufficiently strong to enforce environmental protections would be so strong as to become communist, became active climate-change deniers (p. 38). "Like the tobacco companies who met in New York in 1953, Exxon knew very early on that the burning of fossil fuels was changing the planet's climate" (pp. 34–35). In no way, however, did this hinder their determination to protect their profits by attempting to convince officials and the public that, in the words of U.S. Senator James Inhofe (hardly the most able among his colleagues and unfortunately chair of the Senate Committee on Environment and Public Works) that climate change was simply a hoax. Inhofe may be among the worst, but he is hardly alone. His former staff member, Marc Morano, boasted of using "'nastiness' as a political tactic and having had fun mocking and ridiculing climate scientists." He also—which should come as no surprise—had worked with Rush Limbaugh. Morano said that what he most enjoyed was "going after the individuals, 'cause that is where something lives or dies.'" He would say, "I'm not a scientist, although I do play one on TV occasionally ... Okay, hell, more than occasionally" (p. 43).

The climate change deniers had learned their techniques from decades of pro-tobacco propaganda, and applied them to climate science. "The parallels between the two campaign efforts could not be more striking, since several of the critical players were the same. Among them was Dr. Frederick Seitz who handed out $45 million in grants from the tobacco industry." Ultimately, the tobacco companies found Seitz to be no longer useful to them. One executive in 1989 wrote in a company memo that he was so elderly that he no longer was rational. "Yet in 2001," a dozen years later, "the Heartland Institute one of the principal think tanks funded by the fossil fuel industry to deny the existence of global warming, found him rational enough to author an article," in which he argued that science actually demonstrated that human activities did not affect the planet's temperature" (p. 37).

The accomplishment of the propagandists—of *Lies, Incorporated*—was to create a political debate out of a scientific discussion. The result? They froze the political process. "The industry chooses delay and deceit over change," so that their ability to keep selling earth-damaging products continues undiminished (p. 57).

Their next task was to weave another "well-orchestrated campaign of lies." The topic was healthcare, and in fact "every portion of the Obama White House agenda" (p. 57). It did not begin with Obama, however, but with the Clinton health proposal. One Betsey McCaughey wrote an alarming article in *The New Republic*, "No Exit," in February 1994. It was McCaughey who introduced many of the most alarming lies into the conversation, such as the infamous "death panels," which of course would not have existed under the Clinton plan, and did not and do not and have never existed under "Obamacare." Although her article was built entirely upon falsehoods, conservatives seized upon her allegations, and made the article "the cornerstone of their efforts to defeat the Clinton healthcare plan. In 2006, thirteen years after the publication of 'No Exit,' Franklin Foer, the editor of *The New Republic*, apologized for the article." McCaughey while writing the infamous article had been "receiving guidance from some of the most insidious and self-serving opponents of the health care plan: the tobacco companies" (pp. 62–63).

Regardless, despite McCaughey's record of lies, many of the leading media welcomed her back into the public arena. The occasion was President Obama's Affordable Care Act ("Obamacare"), when the propaganda machine again was employed to attack the president's programs, especially healthcare. The level of truth in the discourse was no better than in the attacks on Clinton's plan. This time there were strong arguments pointing out the falsehoods, but they continued regardless.

Based upon partisan politics, and probably upon the fact that many of the opponents had come to believe their own absurd arguments, House Republicans campaigned against "Obamacare" and voted time and again to repeal it. They did so when Democrats controlled the Senate, and thus there was no chance that Congress would pass the repeal, and they did so after Republicans took control of the Senate, when repeal still had no chance of success because President Obama would simply veto it. It was clear that they were voting for purely symbolic reasons, with no chance at all of success. Part of the reason for such futile votes was pressure from newly elected ultra-conservative members of the House. They wanted a chance to tell their constituents that they "had voted against Obamacare," without regard to the practicality of such a vote. It should be obvious that this is a childish gesture, not an effective way to function in a democracy.

As we all know, they continued even into 2017. At that time, Republicans controlled the presidency; they also controlled both the House and the Senate. Moreover, every Republican had campaigned on "Repeal of Obamacare." Subsequently, that was refined into "Repeal and Replace Obamacare," although the emphasis remained strongly on the "repeal." Despite controlling all the levers of power, Republicans failed twice in their efforts to make government assistance to healthcare availability go away. They growled that they were not done; that eventually they would try again, and would succeed.

Regardless, "conservative" principles, as this example illustrates, are very difficult if not impossible to implement, even when conservatives have complete control. It was obvious, too, to any informed and objective observer, that the results, if they had been successful, would have been catastrophic.

The "replace" part that they ultimately chose would have repealed the program that makes healthcare available almost to the entire population, while replacing it with funds given to the states—funds that explicitly punished the "blue" states that voted for Obama and Clinton, and unduly rewarded the "red" states that did not, especially if they also rejected the expansion of Medicaid that "Obamacare" made possible at almost no cost. For all states, however, those funds within a few years would have vanished. Thus, the "replace" part of "repeal and replace" was pure window-dressing. The effort was simply to save billions of dollars that then could be made available to fund even greater tax reductions for the already extremely wealthy.

No topic seems too arcane to become a target for a campaign of lies. Consider the effects of national debt on growth, and how it, too, became fodder for *Lies, Incorporated*. Of course, the subject did fit neatly into the narrative of Pete Peterson, and of all the advocates of austerity. It also had and has direct effects on people's lives.

In 2010, two prominent economists, Carmen Reinhart and Kenneth Rogoff, published an enormously influential paper, "Growth in a Time of Debt," in *The American Economic Review*. The issue containing the article had "not been subjected to peer review" (p. 74). Although the *AER* is a peer-reviewed journal, its May issues contain papers from conferences and the like that its editors consider important. The Reinhart and Rogoff paper appeared in 2010's May (therefore non-peer-reviewed) issue.

At the time of the paper's publication, the Tea Party movement in the United States was just getting underway ("tea," some adherents said, stood for "taxed enough already"). Progressives for some time had been debating with "deficit hawks." The hawks believed that the way to strengthen the economy was to cut spending, deficits, and debt. They recognized that this would cause pain, and unemployment would increase, creating widespread hardship. Their ideology, however, promised that long-term economic health required short-term pain. It should be noted that the pain would be borne by workers and those not among the economic elite.

The progressives argued, from Keynes, that additional spending, generating deficits, was necessary to stimulate the economy that had plunged with the crash of 2008. They had argued that President Obama's stimulus plan, which was working, should have been greater than the roughly three quarters of a trillion dollars, and that a larger stimulus would have worked better. In defense of the president's stimulus, political realities had worked against a greater stimulus. Very likely they had made a greater one impossible.

Reinhart–Rogoff examined the economies of various countries, and concluded that 90% debt-to-GDP ratio was a tipping point. From that point and higher, debt greatly inhibited economic growth. This conclusion was consistent with Tea Party concerns and with the economic policies of the austerians. Paul Ryan, who was chair of the Budget Committee of the U.S. House, built his highly austere recommendations upon the Reinhart–Rogoff conclusions. Commentators on American news media, American politicians, and many policymakers in other countries under American influence turned to Reinhart–Rogoff to justify severely restrictive economic policies. Some called Reinhart–Rogoff's conclusions "a law of finance" (p. 76).

The Obama administration was able to hold off some of the movement toward austerity in the United States, but not enough to prevent the recovery from being as strong as it should have been.

Elsewhere, it was different, as "liberal economist Dean Baker," noted: "in Europe, R&R's work and its derivatives have been used to justify austerity policies that have pushed the unemployment rate over 10 percent for the euro zone as a whole and above 20 percent in Greece and Spain" (p. 77). Reinhart–Rogoff had meshed with much of the conventional wisdom, and had certainly "taken the world by storm" (p. 78).

Then, in 2012, Thomas Herndon, a graduate student at the University of Massachusetts, received a class assignment to critique and replicate a well-known economics article. He chose Reinhart–Rogoff, and quickly became frustrated. As a mere graduate student reviewing the work of economic superstars, he thought he must be missing something. He could not make the figures work. He communicated with Reinhart and Rogoff, and they gave him their own figures. Herndon easily discovered "several extremely significant problems with Reinhart and Rogoff's work." He and his professors Michael Ash and Robert Pollin, prepared their own paper, published in the *Cambridge Journal of Economics*, which "identified coding errors, selective exclusion of available data and unconventional weighting of summary statistics" in the heralded Reinhart and Rogoff article. Correction of the errors demonstrated that "a debt-to-GDP ratio about 90 percent was simply not the catastrophe Reinhart and Rogoff described" (pp. 78–79).

In fact, the 90% figure had no special significance at all. It may have gained special credence in the United States, because it was only somewhat higher than America's debt-to-GDP ratio at the time.

Reinhart and Rogoff admitted their errors, but continue to maintain that their overall conclusions are correct. They "engaged in a very public battle with their critics, most notably Nobel Laureate Paul Krugman, whom they accused of 'spectacularly uncivil behavior'" (p. 80). This criticism is especially ironic since the Republican Party then chose Donald Trump—known worldwide for his bombastic taunts and his searing condemnations—as its nominee, and succeeded in electing him as president of the United States.

Krugman reminded them, and the public, that reality did not fit the "law of finance" of R & R's study. The crucial difference "'seemed to be whether countries had their own currencies, and borrowed in those currencies.' These nations 'can't run out of money because they can print it if needed, and absent the risk of a cash squeeze, advanced nations are evidently able to carry quite high levels of debt without crisis'" (p. 80).

Lies, Incorporated asks "why, if the facts were so one-sided, if reality did not comport with the basic conclusions of the study, did this piece of economic misinformation infect the political process at such a staggering level?" What was "most appalling," was how it could happen "that a study became accepted fact without any real academic vetting, only to be debunked by a graduate student." Certainly, no one else had even bothered to look at it carefully, since they found the conclusions to be so congenial. "The answer to how it could happen lies in the coordinated effort to cut the debt and its principal benefactor, Peter Peterson." Peterson is a multi-billionaire, and "he supported not only the work of Reinhart and Rogoff but an entire movement focused on putting deficit reduction above all other policy goals" (p. 81).

"Reinhart was appointed a senior fellow at the Peterson Institute for International Economics, funded and chaired by Peterson, in October 2010 and has spoken at Peterson's fiscal summit. Reinhart's partner Rogoff was, and still is, a member of the Peterson Institute's advisory board." The Peterson Institute also "funded and published" Reinhart and Rogoff's book, "*Decade of Debt*" (p. 87).

Despite the revelations regarding the debt study, ideology reigns supreme. Erskine Bowles, who along with the cranky former senator, Alan Simpson, co-chaired the infamous Bowles–Simpson commission on the deficit, "joined Peterson's payroll at Fix the Debt, acknowledged the [R&R] study's flaws but did not shy away or change his ideological stance." He wrote that the discovery of errors did not change "the common sense and my own personal experience in both the public and private sector that when any organization has too much debt that is an enormous risk factor." First, equating the economic circumstances of "any organization" with that of a powerful nation state that controls its own currency, and borrows and pays in that currency, is foolish. It also is dangerous. Second, as *Lies, Incorporated* makes clear, "'Common sense and my own personal experience' is exactly the problem created by conducting research within an ideological bubble: Bowles is happy to accept the conclusions of Reinhart and Rogoff when they conform to his ideology. However, when the conclusions turned out to be wrong," the corrections were irrelevant, could be ignored, and had no effect on Bowles's conclusions (pp. 87–88).

Ideologues, and those under their influence, will "search for research to justify their positions." In the worst instances, they "will simply purchase convenient facts to make their case. They will cherry-pick data or cling to studies with dubious conclusions" (p. 89).

Lies, Incorporated identifies several other such topics, and devotes a chapter to each, and gives detailed analyses of the misrepresentation and outright lies providing the foundation of the propaganda on each topic. These are immigration reform, voter suppression, abortion, and the campaign that ultimately—and only recently—has failed, against same-sex marriage.

Echoes of the latter, though, remain evident in the furor surrounding the use of rest rooms, toilet fixations seeming to have a special fascination to those who are expressing concern just as they did with exactly the same misrepresentations a generation ago when the Equal Rights Amendment ultimately went down to defeat facing just such a charge, among others. It is especially ironic that those on the right, especially the religious right, became obsessed with the specter of a transgender person committing an assault in a women's room, and yet voted enthusiastically for a candidate who not only assaulted women, but bragged about how he "could get away with anything," because he was a celebrity.

The lies that undergird arguments against immigrants, documented and otherwise, are the same that have performed the same function for almost two centuries. They reflect influence from racists and eugenicists. Support for firearms proliferation can arise from similar concerns. It has resulted in complete revision of centuries of constitutional interpretation, and often has reflected the influence of spurious research from such figures as Dr. John Lott, a shill for the firearms industry. Literally at this writing, the morning headlines mention the murder of a young singer as she finished her concert in Florida, followed by the suicide of the attacker. Additionally, there was the massacre of more than 50 in an Orlando nightclub, with some 50 more wounded. Since firearms have become so common, as one would expect, such headlines have also become common. People are outraged at the murders of schoolchildren, but under pressure from the gun lobby and their henchmen no serious policy changes result. Osama bin Laden was correctly named a war criminal, but more people fall victim to firearms in this country than to airline hijackers, yet the carnage brings no liability for those responsible for dangerous policy changes. On the contrary, the law specifically shields gun manufacturers.

All of these topics are relevant to poverty, and voter suppression especially affects those of little means. The intention is political, and the effect is certainly class-based. "Phony accusations of voter fraud are the principal justification behind a variety of voter suppression bills introduced in state legislatures around the country. Though the inevitable result of these laws is the disenfranchisement of minority populations, legislators can deny that is the primary motivation and claim it is coincidental that the laws disproportionally affect minority voters" (p. 134).

As much as any other factor, voter suppression reflects the importance of control of state governments. The Koch brothers and their supporters were shrewd to seek control of the states, and even at times when they have lost at the national level, their influence at least for now remains entrenched at this less visible, but most important, segment of American government.

Regarding abortion, *Lies, Incorporated* examines the ways in which legislators justify restrictive laws as protections for women. Policymakers profess to be against "big government," but take decisions over their bodies away from women and their doctors—assisted by their clergy when appropriate—and give that authority to politicians and government officials. We oppose government regulation of our money, they argue, but not of women's bodies. Additionally, *Lies, Incorporated* reveals the unscientific nature—even the anti-scientific nature—of much of the anti-abortion argument. Abortion is detrimental to women's mental health. Abortion is associated with breast cancer. These and other allegations are not true, but are widely disseminated and may serve to deter women from making their own decisions.

In the final chapter *Lies, Incorporated* asks how the liars can be defeated. This is the least satisfying part of the book, not because what it says is wrong, but because the way to defeat them is so difficult. As I shall argue below, it will depend ultimately on something that good-government groups resisted for so long: absolute partisanship, and an insistence on straight-ticket voting.

Conclusions and Recommendations: Be Partisan!—

The rise of Donald Trump as the victorious candidate of the Republican Party for the 2016 elections reflects the role of irrationality in politics, but since he and the Koch brothers appeared to disagree, it could be interpreted to signify that the Kochtopus had lost control of the party. Rather than be a hopeful development, though, it only suggests that the Kochs do not exercise monolithic influence. They have always experienced setbacks and failures, but that certainly does not suggest that their influence is weak. Even when they fail to influence the choice of president Koch influence remains strong at other levels; that they do not dominate completely does not suggest that their role is not extremely important. Trump is certainly less ideological than the Kochs, or such figures as Ted Cruz, but his emergence as a serious political figure clearly brought chaos which cannot be good for democracy or good government, regardless of what it does to the Republican Party.

To bring American politics closer to at least a semblance of rationality requires something that advocates of "good government" traditionally have opposed. That is strong partisanship and straight-ticket voting. The election results of 2016 make this plain.

For far too long, it was tempting to many to say, "I am tired of voting for the least worst," or to want to "send a message." That is not only self-indulgent, it is impulsive, impatient, and ignores the realities of America's two-party politics. It is especially unrealistic to want to bring a crisis to "shake up the system." No rational system has ever emerged from well-meaning forces who strive to create chaos to force rationality into existence. Chaos breeds only two things: more chaos, or fierce repression.

One cannot be effective politically without recognizing the realities of the system within which one works. When Donald Trump was the Republican nominee, and Hillary Clinton carried the Democratic banner, the way the system works is that no one else could have had a chance at victory. Regardless of anyone's personal preference, it would, regardless, lead to a President Clinton or a President Trump. Votes should have been cast accordingly, despite personal preferences, based on the perception of what was best for the country, not on likes or dislikes, or what made one feel better.

For anyone interested in programs to deal effectively with poverty, with women's issues, with immigration reform, with reducing the economic pressures from student-loan debt and huge healthcare costs, or a great range of progressive interests, refusing to vote for Clinton was to support Trump—no matter what the personal inclination might have been—whether one stayed at home or voted a third party. Bernie Sanders recognized that, and so did Senator Elizabeth Warren when she so eloquently made the same point. Unless one honestly believed that Hillary Clinton would have been no better than Donald Trump—and that is not a realistic evaluation—it was pure self-gratification to do anything other than to work for a Trump defeat, and that required working for a Clinton victory.

It also is understandable to want one of the parties to offer more of what one wants. The Kochs and their allies, and the religious right, recognized how to accomplish their goals. It required patience. They recognized that the way to achieve political goals is to work over a period of years *within one of the two major parties*. Not to work outside the system, and not to take the route of a third party. It was decidedly not to take any action that would lead to the election of the "worst worst," instead of the "least worst," as it did in 2016.

The example of Ralph Nader should be cautionary to anyone who understands the political system. Had he stayed out of Florida in the 2000 elections (Michael Moore in a speech following the election sadly but correctly said just that), it would have saved the country from 8 years of Bush–Cheney. Nader, of course, disagrees, but he is wrong. He could not live with himself if he were to admit to himself that he was responsible.

Trump's advent as a Republican powerhouse was truly momentous. His racist condemnations, his crude characterizations, his own record, and his obvious tactics as a bully, and other characteristics did nothing to stop him. His support was not limited solely to those who simply hate Obama, hate immigrants, disdain women, and wanted to "Take Back America."

His approach to winning was selfish. He has never demonstrated loyalty, and continues to be as ready to attack Republicans as

Democrats. For these, and many other reasons, he may be leading the Republican Party to a great disaster. The results of the 2016 elections could, in 2018, bring a Democratic "wave" election, sweeping the party to a vast victory. Nevertheless, if there were lessons to be learned, they are that however assured a given outcome may seem, nothing can be assured until the votes are fully counted.

The political winds may be shifting. The Republicans have faced the possibility of death as a party twice. In 1936, FDR's overwhelming victory caused some predictions that the Republicans as a party were on the way out. It took two decades for them to work their way back out of the political wilderness, aided by the unpopularity of the Truman administration as it approached 1952, and perhaps especially by the overwhelming popularity of the World War II hero, General Dwight Eisenhower, the GOP's presidential candidate. In 1964, the ill-fated candidacy of Senator Barry Goldwater brought similar predictions. Yet that time, the resurgence took only four years. The party returned to power when Nixon won in an extremely close election in 1968—it subsequently even withstood the Watergate scandals. After that, the GOP continued strong for the rest of the century, and with considerable outside assistance, such as from the Supreme Court, it has remained strong into the twenty-first.

A third near-death experience now could be in the offing. This time, it could be the real demise of the party. Trump as the president is making even Republicans nervous. His appeal may dwindle, as his venom and incompetence become too obvious to dismiss. Before the election, *New York Times* columnist Thomas Friedman, who is known as a spokesman for centrist positions and tends to reflect inside-the-Beltway assumptions, suggested that it was time for the GOP to dissolve.[10] He argued that the party was suffering "moral bankruptcy," and said in effect that it no longer was justified. He said the party was "ethically challenged," and that it is to governing what "Trump University" was to education. This party, he said, no longer has any principles but greed, thirst for power, and opportunism. Clearly, he anticipated a strong Clinton victory, but his conclusion may still be relevant.

For such a bland mainstream figure as Friedman to become so bold is indicative of the crumbling of the Republican Party to a much greater extent than was the case in 1936 and 1964. Friedman said the country needed a center-left party, the Democratic Party, and a rational center-right party, the New Republicans, or whatever it might name itself.

Left unrecognized was that the rightist policies, whenever implemented have never been successful; they have proven not to be viable. Even the supporters of the sainted Ronald Reagan (who admittedly would be far too liberal for today's Republicans) became disenchanted with him. Being unable to bring themselves to attack such a saintly figure, they blamed his advisers who would not "let Reagan be Reagan." The party also turned its collective back on the first Bush (who recognized the need to increase taxes), and later became disenchanted with Bush the son (who, despite his hard-right orientation, recognized that stimulus was vital when the the economy crumbled). The administration of each of these presidents, they began to say, was insufficiently conservative.

Friedman may be correct that the Republicans will vanish (he is correct that they *should*) but it may be that what the country really needs is not two parties, one center-left and the other center-right. Rather, it may need the center-left Democratic Party, and a more liberal party, somewhat to the left of the Democrats.

In the meantime, the strategy that those who seek rational government need to adopt is to stress the need for a strong identification as Democrats. Moreover, there needs to be a huge Democratic turnout to vote. Beyond that, every Democrat needs to vote a straight Democratic ticket. Voting for every Democrat on the ticket in 2018 from members of Congress down to state legislator and points below, is vital. In 2020, it is equally vital to vote for every Democrat from President on down to all offices below. In other words, saving the country requires Democratic wave elections. That is the only way to come close to clearing out the influence of the Kochtopus. It should also hasten the demise of a political party, the Republican Party, that has become dedicated to opposition: opposition to science, to good government, and to the recognition that we are all in this together.

Thus, for the good of all of us, we must work together to make everything work as well as possible. It bears repeating that, for now at least, this means rejecting bipartisanship. The need is for straight-ticket Democratic voting. Make the wave elections happen!

Notes

1 Adapted from an earlier version that appeared in *Poverty and Public Policy* 8 (3) (September 2016).

2 Joey Skidmore, *The Review as Art and Communication* (Newcastle Upon Tyne, UK: Cambridge Scholars' Publishing, 2013).

3 Max J. Skidmore, "Scholarly Support for Social Security: A Political History of Prevailing Beliefs, and of the Growing Number of Works Demonstrating that the 'Conventional' Often Is not 'Wisdom,'" *Poverty and Public Policy* 3 (4).

4 Max J. Skidmore, "Social Security and Its Discontents," *Poverty and Public Policy* 5 (3) (September 2013).

5 Max J. Skidmore, "The People, the Economy and the Issues: A Participant Reports on National 'Town Hall' Meetings on the Deficit," *Poverty and Public Policy* 2 (1) (March 2010).

6 Nancy Altman, *The Truth about Social Security*, forthcoming.

7 Kathleen Romig, "Senate Bill Continues Eroding Social Security Operating Funds," *Blog Post,* Center on Budget and Policy Priorities (p June 2016); reprinted by permission.

8   Max J. Skidmore, "Anti-Government Is Not the Solution to Our Problem, Anti-Government IS the Problem: Presidential Response to Natural Disasters, San Francisco to Katrina," *Journal of Risk, Hazards, and Crisis in Public Policy* 3 (4) (December 2012).

9   Theodore Roosevelt, *An Autobiography* (New York: A Da Capo Press Reprint, 1913), 67.

10 Thomas Friedman, "Dump G.O.P. for a Grand New Party," *New York Times*, June 8, 2016.

CHAPTER 4
POLICY INSIGHTS FROM PARTY HISTORY[1]

Lewis L. Gould, *The Republicans: A History of the Grand Old Party*, New York, Oxford University Press, 2014.

Nancy MacLean, *Democracy in Chains: The Deep History of the Radical Right's Stealth Plan for America*, New York: Viking, 2017.

Heather Cox Richardson, *To Make Men Free: A History of the Republican Party*, New York: Basic Books, 2014.

The political system of the United States has been characterized by the existence of two major political parties for most of its existence: a two-party system that has indelibly influenced America's political institutions, and its political development. Although it may not always be clear during the discussion that follows, it should be recognized that each of the dominant parties has maintained a distinct character, and also that each one also has contained varied currents. At its most monolithic, each party has always contained within itself at least some who disagree.

The older of the two existing parties, the Democratic Party, began during the presidency of Andrew Jackson elected first in 1828 and again in 1832. The party that emerged to oppose Jackson's emphasis on limited national government plus an active and energetic executive was the short-lived Whig Party. Within about two decades, that anti-Jackson party had dissipated, and was no more.

The Republican Party traces its beginnings to 1854. Although the party was not abolitionist, the Republicans had coalesced around a single goal related to slavery: they were determined to restrict the system's spread into the territories. In 1856, the Republicans ran John C. Fremont as their first presidential candidate, but he lost to James Buchanan, the Democrat. A mere four years later, six years after their Republican Party's formation, they elected their first president, Abraham Lincoln. Republicans then remained for the most part dominant until the election of Democrat Franklin D. Roosevelt, in 1932.

From the Republican victory in 1860 until the party's crushing defeat in 1932, only two Democrats held the presidency: Grover Cleveland, for two nonconsecutive terms (elected in 1884, defeated in 1888, and elected again in 1892), and Woodrow Wilson elected for two terms in 1912 and 1916. However much the Republicans came to ally themselves with big business, on the issue of black civil rights their record for decades—however flawed—remained far better than that of the Democrats. This began to change following the election in 1932 of Franklin D. Roosevelt. As FDR implemented his "New Deal" from 1933 onward, the Democratic Party slowly began its turn toward civil rights. This reorientation brought disquiet to the party's powerful southern wing in the old "Solid South," but nonetheless it continued. Ultimately, after victories by determined civil rights activists, it brought a shift in the south's orientation. Its racist Democrats became racist Republicans, and moved overwhelmingly into the Republican Party.

At the Democratic Party's formation and for a time thereafter, the Democrats were often known simply as "the Democracy." Jackson, himself, the party's first president was also the first president openly to avow political partisanship, even though he considered himself to be an old Jeffersonian. The Founders, Thomas Jefferson included, although often acting in partisan ways, opposed political parties, but by Jackson's time, it gradually had come to seem obvious that parties were both inevitable, and perhaps even desirable.

Regardless of the rather nebulous background of parties prior to the formal emergence of the Democratic Party, that party long has traced its lineage beyond Jackson to Jefferson. Whatever the merits of that genealogy, it is clear that what came to be the Democratic Party emerged from elements that made up the Jeffersonian Republicans. It also is clear, that despite the assertion by the Jeffersonian Republicans of the "Rights of Man" arguments (today we would say simply "human rights"), and despite Jefferson's primary authorship of the marvelous Declaration of Independence, the Jeffersonian Republicans were the party of slavery. The members of the short-lived Federalist Party, aristocratic or not, were likely to be considerably more anti-slavery than were the largely southern Jeffersonians.

By 1820, the Federalist Party was dead. After the fading away over the next decade or so of the Jeffersonian Republicans, the newly emerged Democratic Party inherited the role as the primary party of slavery. The powerful slavery impulse within the party ultimately overwhelmed the strong unionist focus that had characterized Jackson and his followers, and the Democratic Party became the party of rebellion and secession. Following the Civil War, the Democrats were the party of segregation and "Jim Crow" restrictions on black citizens, and to some extent in the south, restrictions on Republicans as well. This began to change, slowly, with the New Deal in the 1930s, and more rapidly in the 1940s with Harry Truman's desegregation of U.S. military forces and his efforts to mandate fair housing. The major breakthroughs thereafter began with the U.S. Supreme Court's unanimous *Brown* v. *Board of Education* decision in 1954, that outlawed racial segregation in the public schools, the culmination of which was the massive civil rights demonstration of 1963 in Washington, D.C. at which Dr. Martin Luther King gave his "I Have a Dream" address. Courageous and determined efforts by civil rights groups had brought demonstrations through the country since the 1954 decision, even in the deepest parts of the south. Then, in 1964, came Lyndon Johnson's Civil Rights Act, followed by his Voting Rights Act of 1965.

Concerted opposition to civil rights was driving the solid Democratic south into the arms of the waiting Republicans, who ultimately adopted "southern strategies," voter suppression, and other repressive measures. Thus, they supplanted the Democrats as the party that acted as though it had a southern heritage. Eventually, Republicans began to impose a newer and more subtle form of Jim Crow. The party had departed from its founding—civil rights— principles, and permitted the waiting Democrats (with all their own faults) to become more the party of equality.

Because of its intricate, and highly inconsistent, history, the American Republican Party presents a fascinating subject for the student of this country's society and culture. In fact, a study of the history of that party alone is sufficient to provide insights that can serve as the basis for numerous generalizations regarding the United States as a whole. Two recent histories of the party provide foundations for deep interpretations of the driving factors of American politics. Each is thoughtful and well researched. Each is essential reading for the student interested in how America functions. Paradoxically, each—while remaining complementary and not really contradictory—is considerably at variance with the other. It is unfortunate that both of these works came out too soon to take note of the Donald Trump phenomenon. It is safe to say, though, that both authors, however they differ in interpretation, describe a situation from which such a political earthquake—revealing the fragile nature of the most fundamental institutions and safeguards that America had crafted and evolved beyond two centuries and into a third—might have been anticipated. Looking deeply at that earthquake is a third book, McLean's *Democracy in Chains*. It can be read somewhat as a culmination of the other two, and certainly as adding considerably to them—without being an actual party history.

Heather Cox Richardson provides an unusual and intriguing look at that history in *To Make Men Free*, and she does so brilliantly. As she reads the party's history, it was founded in radicalism, experienced backlash leading it to reaction, reverted back to reform, and then again to the far right. The GOP, she says, experiences "ongoing renegotiation of the party's—and the nation's—central unresolved problem: the profound tension between America's two fundamental beliefs, equality of opportunity and protection of property."[2] As with the other works listed above, the presentation here of this one is not to indicate that it is definitive, nor that it is flawless, but that it is highly suggestive, and offers much potential insight.

Richardson describes the vast swings that have characterized the Republican Party. On the one hand, we find the post-Civil War era that Reconstruction scholar Douglas Egerton has called "most progressive period in American history,"[3] followed a generation later by the Progressive era dominated by Theodore Roosevelt. On the other hand, in a repudiation of its heritage, is the right-wing extremism of the current party now dominated by Donald Trump. Trump came along too late for Richardson to take note of him, but his success grew out of practices that began to take root with Nixon and Reagan, which reflected tendencies that long predated those two quite significant presidents.

Richardson identifies the swings as regular progressions. Humanitarian activism generates resistance and reaction from propertied interests that lead to upward transfers of wealth. Extreme inequality then brings new reform elements, and another shift toward the interests of the people. There can be no doubt that these swings have taken place, although it is less clear that they are part of a naturally recurring cycle. Along with most scholars who purport to identify regularly recurring cycles in human affairs, she perhaps strains somewhat to make her case. An example may be when she classes Eisenhower as among the progressives. To be sure, his "modern Republicanism" did come to terms with the New Deal and preserve its reforms. Eisenhower even signed into law disability benefits through the Social Security system, an enormous social advance, and a costly one. Nevertheless, although Eisenhower was pragmatic and realistic, and although he could be persuaded to accept generous social programs, he was inherently conservative, and had to be convinced that whatever he was approving was not "socialism." For instance, he opposed programs that ultimately led to Medicare, and undoubtedly was reluctant in his support for civil rights. Regardless, it is certainly clear that Eisenhower was far to the left of the Bushes, especially the younger Bush, and of Trump.

In her focus on Lincoln, TR, and Eisenhower Richardson also ignores much recent historical analysis that demonstrates the progressive policies of other Republicans of the massively misinterpreted "Gilded Age" era, especially Grant and Benjamin Harrison.[4]

Richardson's writing, though, is clear and cogent. Regardless of the questions that may arise regarding details, her thought also is compelling. To avoid distorting her argument, it is well to quote her own words. Throughout the party's history, she says "Republicans have swung from one pole to another: sometimes they have been leftists, sometimes reactionaries. Today, once again the Republican Party has positioned itself on the far right. How did the Republican Party—the party of Abraham Lincoln, Theodore Roosevelt, and Dwight D. Eisenhower—become the party of today?"[5]

As indicated, the Party was founded in 1854, determined to prevent the spread of slavery. It elected its first president 6 years later, the most outstanding of all our presidents, Abraham Lincoln. Lincoln expanded the purposes of the Republican Party to work toward equality, to encourage free labor, to provide education and land to the people, and to prevent vast disparities of wealth. During his presidency, Lincoln not only attacked slavery and worked to abolish it with the Thirteenth Amendment, but he signed into law the Homestead Act, to provide land to Americans; the first income tax, to help fund the Civil War and guard against huge accumulations of wealth; and the Morrill Act, that established land-grant universities, so that higher education would not be limited to the wealthy. The Republicans passed all these laws, and worked for racial justice as well.

After Lincoln's tragic assassination and the disastrous presidency of his successor Andrew Johnson, who worked deliberately to undercut Reconstruction, the Republican Party despite the valiant efforts of President Grant seemed to tire of its reform activities, and developed a new wing. Its members (ironically, when considering today's terminology) called themselves Liberal Republicans. That these Republicans were more interested in protecting property than in equality puts it mildly. They had no interest at all in civil rights for the new American citizens of African descent. As the nineteenth century progressed, their interest in civil rights continued to wane, but not their interest in protecting the affluent. They passed laws that permitted wealth to accumulate at the top to such an extent that by the end of the century, there arose another protest within the Party.

This was the Progressive movement, led by Theodore Roosevelt. TR recognized that government had to be strong to protect Americans against the new corporations and the wealthy "robber barons," as we think of them today, or as he described them, "malefactors of great wealth." Progressivism continued as a major force through the twentieth century's first two decades, and then once more a conservative reaction took place.

The 1920s brought the administrations of Warren Harding, Calvin Coolidge, and Herbert Hoover. They were devoted to keeping government small and taxes low, while avoiding regulation, and boosting business. The result, again, was a flow of money upward and a great concentration of wealth, followed by the Great Depression that began in 1929.

As an anomaly, perhaps, one should recognize that with all its faults, even during its periods of reaction, from the Civil War until the beginning of the New Deal, the Republican Party was better than the Democratic Party with regard to civil rights for Americans of African descent. The Democratic Party, of course, rested to a considerable extent on the Solid South, which provided it with an equally solid, but rigidly segregated, base. The early twentieth century was hardly a time of civil rights anywhere in America, but just as the Republican presidents of the nineteenth century—Lincoln, Grant, Hayes, Arthur, Garfield, Benjamin Harrison, and McKinley—were far better on the issue than was the Democrat, Cleveland (or, certainly, the Democrat elected on the "Union Ticket," with Lincoln, Andrew Johnson); so, too were the early twentieth-century Republicans—Theodore Roosevelt, Taft, Harding, and possibly Coolidge and Hoover—considerably better than the only Democrat of the period, the progressive, but southern and racist, President Woodrow Wilson. This changed, of course, with the New Deal, when the Democrats (other than their southern wing) became the friendlier of the two parties to civil rights. This is not to say that Franklin D. Roosevelt was a pioneer on the subject, but his New Deal did adopt measures that at least in a limited way began to erode some of the rigid patterns of segregation and racial discrimination.

With FDR's new Democratic administration and his New Deal, and with the example before them of the Progressive Republicans of a generation before, again government turned its attention to regular citizens, not merely the wealthy. Far more than before, it began to tax to provide benefits, and to regulate business in the interest of the public good. As before, such policies benefited the public, and outraged the wealthy. This time, the Republicans stayed away from progressive policies. In 1936, their candidate for president, Kansas Governor Alf Landon, called the new Social Security System "a cruel hoax." FDR won an enormous landslide, carrying every state except Maine and Vermont. World War II absorbed the reform momentum, but the New Deal continued through the Truman administration. Truman was thwarted in his efforts to expand it considerably, but even in the face of a Congress dominated by Republicans and southern Democrats, he managed to protect FDR's gains. Astonishingly, considering the existing political dynamics and the widespread racism throughout the country, he even succeeded, by executive order, in banning racial discrimination in the military.

Conservatives began to muster their forces quietly, and without publicity. When the Republicans regained power after the election in 1952 of Dwight Eisenhower, the party was split between the Old Guard, under the leadership of Senator Robert A. Taft, and the moderates under Eisenhower. Eisenhower spoke of "modern republicanism," and argued that the New Deal programs were part of the American way of Life, and must be protected. He signed into law disability benefits, a huge new program added to the Social Security System.

The Old Guard evolved into the Movement Conservatives, continued to preach minimal government, isolationism, and unrestrained business. Now, they often like to call themselves "constitutional conservatives," as though their constitutional interpretations were the only ones consistent with the desires of "the Founders," and as though the Founders—including both of the great antagonists Jefferson and Hamilton, for example—were unanimous in their interpretations. Movement conservatives even threw their weight in the 1950s behind the proposed Bricker Amendment to the Constitution, which to his great credit President Eisenhower behind the scenes used his political skills to scuttle. This would have required every treaty to be consistent with every American law, federal, state, or presumably even local. That would have meant that every jurisdiction—or at least every state—could have challenged a treaty, and that would have relegated the government of the United States to impotence. It would have thrown America back into a confederacy, such as existed under the Articles of Confederation. The fascination with their view of "states' rights" among the movement conservatives is just that: a fascination with confederacies, rather than with a federal government. Their constitutional approach, as a matter of fact, reflects more the views of those who opposed the Constitution, than of the Founders who ratified and implemented it.

America's national experience with confederations, of course, has been disastrous. They fail. The scheme under the Articles of Confederation did so spectacularly, and the Confederate States of America—formed to destroy the federal system of the Union and preserve slavery—failed most spectacularly still. Nevertheless, the romantic sentiment among movement conservatives for confederacies and states' rights continues today, even to the extent of advocating measures that would permit states to overrule the national government. It also would take selection of U.S. senators away from a state's people and give it back to its legislature. This has become a fairly well-developed movement to repeal the seventeenth Amendment—the amendment that gave the people the vote for senators—and at political science meetings, there frequently are panels on "federalism" that reflect this sentiment; a sentiment clearly based upon the assumption that the sense of a state can be expressed only by its legislature; not by its courts, by its governor, or (oddly) even by its people acting directly.

Movement conservatives were a major force in the administration of Richard Nixon. Nixon, though, on the other hand did work for some social programs, going so far as to propose a guaranteed annual income—playing both sides—while courting the reactionaries with his "southern strategy," using coded appeals to the racist elements who made up much of its membership.

The reaction against regulation continued, and the movement conservatives coalesced around the charismatic figure of a former movie actor, Ronald Reagan. In 1980, he was elected to the presidency. Reagan began his campaign in Philadelphia, Mississippi, where civil rights workers had been murdered during their struggles for social justice. This was a not-so-subtle appeal to racists, continuing and even expanding, Nixon's southern strategy. In his startling inaugural address, Reagan remarked that government was not the solution to the problem, government was the problem.

He immediately set out to reduce regulations, eliminate the Fairness Doctrine in broadcasting (enabling the later developments of Fox News as a conduit for Republican propaganda, and extremist talk radio), attack environmentalists as meddlers, and seek to undo Social Security. Reagan also slashed taxes, which led his party to a decades-long obsession: led by movement conservatives, Republicans developed hostility to the very idea of taxation itself. To be sure, Reagan did fail to eliminate Social Security—although he did cut benefits and eliminated others—and after having created a backlash from the public, he promised never again to attack the program. He remained true to his word on Social Security, but otherwise continued to pursue the rest of his agenda. To show his disdain for environmentalists, he ordered the solar panels that President Carter had installed on the White House roof removed (President Obama later restored them; what will happen to them now is anyone's guess).

Movement conservatives dominated the administrations of Reagan and especially George W. Bush—where they were joined by the internationally aggressive "Neo-conservatives"; that is, Straussians (purported followers of the teachings of the late Leo Strauss). Movement conservatives were instrumental in shaping policies among the congressional Republicans after Newt Gingrich, Tom DeLay, later Mitch McConnell, and others came to power. The new leaders welcomed the extreme fringes into the party, made alliances with the most fervent elements of the fundamentalist evangelicals who sought and still seek to establish a theocracy in the United States, and proceeded otherwise to throw off all restraints that had characterized party politics in modern America. The result was furious hatred for Bill and especially Hillary Clinton; ultimately with the actual impeachment of a president.

When the younger Bush came to power, although he had campaigned as a relative moderate, he governed as a movement conservative, and especially in foreign affairs gave prominence to the Straussian "neoconservatives." His domestic policy brought reductions of regulations and sharp lowering of taxes, bringing another upward rush of income, especially to the very top. This—despite the dogma that tax cuts and untrammeled business brings trickle-down and prosperity for all—was followed, as it has tended to be throughout history, by another economic crash; this time it was the greatest economic disaster since the Great Depression itself.

The movement conservatives' outrage peaked when Barack Obama, whom they condemned as a foreigner and a radical—and by some even as the antichrist—became president. Shortly before he left office after his two terms, President Obama joked about a southern evangelist who said that he and Hillary Clinton were "demons," and that anyone near them could smell sulfur. Obama sniffed his wrist, laughed, and said, "Not so"!

The movement conservatives have scorned science, and cultivated a rejection of facts. In fact, they preach that facts are irrelevant. They glory in anti-intellectualism, anti-rationality, and an absolute rejection of reality. This has become too obvious to ignore in the months since President Obama left office.

Southern reactionaries after the Civil War resented the abolition of slavery, and set the tone for much of the subsequent racism in this country. They were the intellectual grandparents and parents of the movement conservatives, who remain convinced that the key to utopia is minimal government, no regulation, and little or no taxation. Accordingly, they continue to attack our government of the people as if it were an alien force imposed upon us.

They give ample evidence of being unwilling to follow the rules of the game or accept any restrictions on their behavior. They do whatever they believe will help them win—no holds barred. Unable to appeal to a majority of the people, they admit to going beyond gerrymandering, and to trying to suppress the vote. This explains all the furor about "phony voters." For all practical purposes, such voters do not exist, but conservatives use them to justify requirements for identification laws, and other obstructions. They sometimes even direct police efforts to halt voter registration—as took place in 2016 in Vice President Pence's own state of Indiana, when he was governor. Pence bragged about it. A trump campaign official, similarly, bragged during the campaign about "three major voter suppression operations underway." He said the campaign was "targeting young white liberals, young women, and black voters with negative ads focused on Hillary Clinton's politics, Bill Clinton's past, and comments Clinton made in the 1990s about black criminals." That isn't really "voter suppression," but is part of the same effort. Conservative efforts themselves at least bordered on the criminal when they engaged in "poll watching," and employed off-duty police officers and deputies, in uniform and armed, to intimidate voters at the polls in minority precincts.

Thus, there should have been little or no surprise, that with the movement conservative takeover of the Republican Party, that party in 2016 shamelessly nominated a boisterous vulgarian swindler, who demeans women, minorities, and the handicapped, who threatened one-person rule, who raged that any election that did not select him would have been "rigged," and who loudly asserted that he knew more than the experts on almost any subject under discussion (e.g., more than the generals about ISIS). In view of the character of the campaign—reflecting the conditioning of a quarter century of vilification of Hillary Clinton, computer hacking directed against her, the actions of foreign powers, astonishing comments by the director of the FBI, and more—in retrospect, it might have been expected that Trump would be victorious.

It should also have been no surprise that major Republicans during the campaign—Senators John McCain (who knew better) and Ted Cruz (who perhaps did not)—threatened, if they continued to have congressional majorities, to refuse confirmation for any judicial nomination (perhaps all nominations for all positions) by a President Hillary Clinton for all the years she held office if elected. They also (see Jason Chaffetz, who was a U.S. representative from Utah) gleefully anticipated 4 years of solid investigations of a President Clinton, as soon as she took office, in the hopes of eliminating the effectiveness of another branch, the executive, if under the control of the other party. There was even talk of impeaching Clinton before she took office. Of course that could not have resulted in her removal unless two thirds of the Senate were to have voted for guilt to remove her, but it indicates how destructive are the forces that led and are leading one of our two major parties. With the Trump victory those threats became moot, but they remain in the historical record.

Donald Trump did not create the current political chaos. Rather, it is the natural outcome of sick tendencies that American conservatives nurtured, as they assumed that they could gain and keep power by dominating the Republican Party, and then could control the forces they had encouraged, even the most extreme. Those forces now are consuming the Party. Left unchecked, they soon could be consuming the fabric of American constitutional government, and they begin by dismantling the legislation designed to protect the most needy.

To reiterate, Richardson notes that the path Republicans have taken is far from straightforward. "Since its formation in the 1850s, the party has, in three different eras, swung from one end of the political spectrum to the other. In each of these cycles, Republicans have replayed the same pattern. In their progressive periods they have expanded the vote, regulated business, and raised taxes. As a result, wealth became widely distributed and the economy strong." After each progressive period, though, there has been "a backlash from within its own ranks. After Lincoln, and after Roosevelt and Eisenhower as well, Republican leaders gradually turned against their own reforms in favor of protecting the interests of the rich. Their argument was always that taxes redistribute wealth, interfering with the fundamental 'right to property.' Adamant that hardworking white men not see their fortunes transferred to lazy African Americans and immigrants, they cut funding for education and social welfare programs. As Republican policy shifted, and the machinery of government was enlisted to promote big business, wealth moved upward."[6]

One should note that this has been a deliberate policy of the Republican Party since the election of Ronald Reagan as president. Despite their scorn for "wealth redistribution," modern Republicans have indulged in a frenzy of redistribution that one can describe legitimately as "furious." They do not recognize it as the dreaded "socialism," however, because it purposely is a distribution upward—an inverted socialism for the rich—and sharply away from those who are most needy.

As Richardson recognizes—but the ideologues of the right do not—the result of these policies is consistent: "each time," she says, "these periods of reaction were followed by a devastating economic crash." Moreover, "there is nothing at all random about the Republicans' ideological shifts. They reflect the GOP's ongoing renegotiation of the party's—and the nation's—central unresolved problem: the profound tension between America's two fundamental beliefs, equality of opportunity and protection of property."

In a truly deep reading of American political history, she describes the genesis of this tension as it resulted early in the westward migration, into what became Kentucky, long before the Republican Party's formation. Immediately after the Revolution, "Americans rushed to lay claim to the region's riches. Once there, they quickly discovered that equality was not the inevitable result of economic freedom." That is a massive understatement. "Some men settled on better land than others; some had family money; some were just lucky, and quickly those men accumulated more than others." When wealth built up, it brought political power, "which they used to secure legislation that promoted their interests at the expense of poorer settlers. They justified their actions with the Constitution's mandate that property must be protected." The result was prolonged, or even exacerbated, inequality, because the laws they enacted "circumscribed other men's ability to rise; and wealth moved upward."[7]

At the same time, there were national leaders who recognized what was happening. Even under the Articles of Confederation, which provided almost no power to the center and kept virtually all authority at the state level, they managed to pass the Northwest Ordinance of 1787, "which was designed to prevent" the wealthy from dominating others. Those who wrote the Ordinance, including Thomas Jefferson, "outlawed both primogeniture and slavery," systems that led directly to the concentration of wealth. Unfortunately, that ordinance did not cover what then was the southwest, the area that came to include such states as Alabama, Mississippi, Arkansas, Tennessee, Kentucky, and western Florida. "Over the next fifty years, as a handful of wealthy slave owners tightened a stranglehold on the South, it remained possible for poor men to rise in the northern lands protected by the Northwest Ordinance." The results "were stark. By the beginning of the Civil War, the protection of equality in the north and of property in the south had led to vigorous society outside the south, while inside the south, the wealthy few oppressed the remainder, free as well as slave."[8]

Southern power holders were well aware that their system was unstable; that its continuation "depended upon keeping those at the bottom of society from political power."[9] Thus, it depended upon retaining and preserving massive amounts of poverty. Southerners were furious when the new Republican Party pushed back against the power of the wealthy slaveholders. They knew they were under attack when President Lincoln made his famous comment that Republicans were "for both the *man* and the *dollar*; but in cases of conflict, the man *before* the dollar."[10]

This comment that so inspired Republicans then, now outrages them, as they have gone fully to the side of the wealthy, while cynically cultivating the "common man" by convincing many that such things as protecting them from healthcare preserve his "freedom." Despite some questionable conclusions—for example, that Lincoln was complicit in removing Vice President Hamlin from the ticket in 1864 to be replaced by Andrew Johnson—Richardson provides a sound assessment of the increasing commitment to wealth of the Republican Party for the next few decades. She relies on historical fact in dealing with Grant, for example, instead of "received wisdom" (such information is indeed "received," but often is far from wise). She thus avoids the unjustified condemnation that has dominated so much writing about Grant, and still unduly influences popular opinion. Undoubtedly, she is deft in tracing the tension in the party between emphasizing equal rights, on the one hand, and the defense of property and unlimited accumulation of wealth, on the other. It is unfortunate that her book came before the great upheaval of Donald Trump, and the travesty that has replaced one of America's two major political parties.

It is well to remember that those elements of the American right now branded as "Movement Conservatives," had always been present, but for most of the last few decades had been known—accurately—as right wing extremists. Beginning with Goldwater's abortive 1964 run for the presidency, their influence began truly to take root in the "Southern Strategy," of the Nixon administration, and the increasing movement toward the right, especially the southern right, that came with the election of Ronald Reagan—which included intensification of that southern strategy. Reagan, himself, shortly before his nomination had represented the far-right fringe of the Republican Party. He was more pragmatic than his rhetoric had promised—although current Republicans have sanctified him and have forgotten that when he was in office, they chanted "Let Reagan be Reagan," blaming his advisers for not "letting" President Reagan be himself. Nevertheless, the movement conservatives gained strength in his administration, and have become ever stronger since, financed by billions of dollars from the Koch Brothers and others, buttressing the political ideology promulgated by the late economist, James M. Buchanan (who, intellectually, whether or not he actually claimed discipleship, was largely the reincarnation of long-dead racist and anti-democratic extremist, John C. Calhoun). They cleansed the party of liberals, and even moderates, revealing their highly ideological nature by adoption of a label of scorn to apply to those of inadequate ideological purity: RINO; that is, Republican in name only.

"If they hated RINOs, Movement Conservatives were apoplectic about Democrats, *those Liberals who were pushing America toward socialism!*" (emphasis supplied). "They worried that Clinton would find a way to erase the gains of the Reagan years. They had spent forty years fighting 'statism.'" Literally, of course, so-called "statism," is simply the belief that government has some utility beyond merely protecting property. The public had little strong concern about taxes, Richardson points out, but it was key to the movement conservatives' outrage. Their "rhetoric against taxes continued to mount as they pushed supply-side economics. Promising to slash budgets and cut taxes, regardless of the effect on state and local governments, was almost always a recipe for victory." Nevertheless, their talking points were unrelated to reality. They "continued to insist that social welfare was simply Democratic vote buying. When Clinton proposed a national healthcare plan, they worried that healthcare benefits would cement more voters to the Democrats, and they attacked it with the same sort of vicious misrepresentation that had worked in the Willie Horton ad." They did not stop there, however. They opposed protecting women against domestic violence "as an attempt to create more government jobs." They charged that support for education was nothing more than "a payoff for teachers' unions or a plot to indoctrinate children into Liberal ideas. Movement Conservatives called for 'school choice', the privatization of the educational system, or home schooling to guarantee children's moral safety. Support for affirmative action was 'reverse discrimination'; Movement Conservatives suggested that the real people at risk in America were white men."[11] Ultimately, as we all remember they unleashed the "hydrogen bomb of American politics." That is, they succeeded in impeaching President Clinton—and for nothing remotely related to the performance of his official duties. They could not convict him in the Senate, though. Impeachment requires only a majority vote in the House, but Senate conviction requires a vote of two thirds. With some Republicans joining with Democrats, the Movement Conservatives could not even muster a majority of the vote in the upper chamber.

It is unfortunate, as indicated above, that Richardson's study came too early to deal with the Trump phenomenon. Nevertheless, it is sufficiently recent to take note of the Obama election, and as she said, that "revealed the hollow core of the twenty-first century Republican Party. Immediately," she wrote, "opponents shrieked that the president-elect was a socialist or a communist. They denied that he had been fairly elected, and they denied that he was an American, insisting" against clear and compelling evidence, it should be pointed out, that "he was born in Kenya and was therefore constitutionally barred from becoming president"[12] (p. 340). Donald Trump was at the heart of this "birther" movement that spread the easily disproven lie that Obama was not a natural born American citizen.

It was astonishing that many adherents of one of America's two major political parties, apparently convincing themselves, fulminated that the new president was "stupid, uneducated, inexperienced," and that he had been elected "only because he had represented a special interest." The propaganda they propagated as often as not was "hideous," and "racist." In Barack Obama, "all the themes Republican leaders had developed since the 1850s came together." He was well educated, even having been editor of the *Harvard Law Review*; he was intelligent. Moreover, he had worked diligently to rise. He "was the embodiment of the dream Lincoln had articulated, Theodore Roosevelt had adapted to the era of industrialism, and Eisenhower had formulated for the modern world." Obama was the "progressive Republican's dream," but he had African ancestry, and was the Old South's "nightmare come to life: a black man in charge, with every intention of using the government to help 'mudsills.' Obama was also the worst fear of late nineteenth and early twentieth-century Republicans. A Democrat who wanted to rein in business"[13] (pp. 340–341).

Although there has been much critical praise for *To Make Men Free*, some reviewers have called Richardson's work excessively partisan. On the contrary, it describes Republicans not only at their worst, but also at their best. It is difficult, if not impossible, to present a realistic portrayal of recent Republicans without appearing harsh; hence, partisan. The truth at times can be painful. This is one of those times.

Reviewers have been less likely to hurl the charge of partisanship at Lewis Gould's fine, and well-accepted, work, *The Republicans: A History of the Grand Old Party*, despite his having been at least as harsh in his judgment as Richardson. Part of the reason for this is that the first edition was published in 2003. The reviews generally refer to the original version that had yet to take note of the deep irrationality that had come to characterize the party, and they tend to praise the book's even-handed approach. Moreover, *The Republicans* as yet seems not to have attracted the notice of readers from the far right who pounce on anything they view as critical. One review did say that the work was excellent up until its treatment of the party after the Reagan presidency, but after that point, it became almost a diatribe "against the Party due to its growing conservatism" (William A. Woolley on the Amazon website; https://www.amazon.com/Republicans-History-Grand-Old-Party-ebook/dp/B00MBEQSG8/ref=sr_1_2?ie=UTF8&qid=1503935689&sr=8-2&keywords=Gould%2C+History+of+the+Republican). That, of course, is the position that modern "conservatives" would be quick to adopt, but it is wrong.

The highly critical tone (the "near diatribe" that Woolley cites) has nothing to do with conservatism. Rather Gould noted the party's rush to become anti-intellectual and reject science, reason, and evidence as well as its decision "that democratic procedures should no longer constrain its behavior," leading, as he put it, to "a major breakdown in how American politics works."[14] The rejection of democratic procedures—such as the urgency with which recent Republicans have adopted restriction after restriction to suppress the vote of any population that they view as likely to support Democrats—has nothing to do with "conservatism," nor with any political position other than urge to secure and maintain political power.

The thrust of Gould's analysis overall remains the same in the revised (2014) edition as it was in the original. The Republican Party's very founding was based on human freedom, prosperity for the people, and a vision for the future. The Democratic Party, to be sure, had expanded democracy, and had been organized to a large extent to speak up for the "forgotten man."

Its interpretation of the common man, though, was just that. It did not include women (nor did most early Republicans, of course), and was interested only in a distinct segment of the dispossessed. Not only did that segment not include slaves, the Democratic Party had come to be largely an advocate for the southern position, and the southern position had become extreme. No longer did southerners agree that slavery was an unfortunate evil that could be contained; no longer did they hope for its ultimate elimination. Instead, the south had become aggressive, insisting that slavery spread virtually without limit. Moreover, that slaveholding south had come for the most part to speak through the Democratic Party.

Thus, at the Republican Party's formation, it perceived the Democrats as representing a "fundamentally different" governing commitment. "The historical record shows that through more than a century and a half of its existence, the Republican Party has viewed the world of American politics as an arena in which it is entitled to govern against a partisan rival that has always been out of the national mainstream." Thus, "Republicans have always believed that they have an inalienable right to hold power because of their record and their values." The Democrats, on the other hand, supported a south that advocated human bondage, the destruction of the American Union through secession, and the rejection of the values of the Declaration of Independence. Democrats therefore could not be trusted. Of course, "many Democrats supported the war effort, but others did not." In fact, it is understandable that the Republican Party formed around a feeling—and often an actual idea—that "Democrats had not just flirted with treason: they had consorted with the enemy."[15]

To add to the mix, Gould looks at the functioning of the parties at the end of the nineteenth century and into the early twentieth. "Under leaders like William Jennings Bryan, the Democrats had emphasized the virtues of emotion over reason, conversion over persuasion, religion over science." On the other hand, "between 1865 and 1940 the Republicans had been the organization of intellectuals and the well educated (alongside the rank and file, of course),"[16] and as such tended to view Democrats with disdain. During the First World War, they also became concerned about "Bolshevism and other radical ideologies" that were emerging in Europe. "Republicans saw Democratic programs under Woodrow Wilson as offshoots of these noxious systems. In 1920, addressing the Republican Convention, Henry Cabot Lodge said: 'Mr. Wilson stands for a theory of administration and government which is not American,'" and to be sure, Wilson, under wartime pressures, had seized power and crushed civil liberties. Later, "the questioning of Democratic loyalty returned and became more intense during the New Deal of Franklin D. Roosevelt. Voices on the right asserted that the entire administration of FDR was controlled by the Kremlin."[17]

Just as slavery was the major issue that cut through nearly all others from the founding until the Civil War, so too after the War has race continued to dominate. Republican attitudes could deny legitimacy to Democrats because of their support for slavery, and later, both because of their support for segregation, and their anti-intellectualism. As the Democrats evolved to become the party most friendly to civil rights, however, the Republicans "sensed a bounty of white votes in the states of the old Confederacy. Under Dwight D. Eisenhower and then Richard Nixon, Republicans reaped a rich harvest of white support, and the party dominated the presidency in the 1970s and 1980s." They previously had taken "justified pride in their record in the nineteenth century of freeing the slaves and enacting the Reconstruction amendments to the Constitution. Democrats had taken an unduly long time to discard their racist past. In the 1960s and 1970s, however, the parties passed each other in opposite directions. The party of Kennedy and Lyndon Johnson became as identified with the aspirations of African Americans as previous members of the party had been with keeping alive segregation and discrimination."

As a result of these shifts, Republicans "found reasons to champion the cause of white southerners and like-minded northerners in the service of victory at the polls and the opportunity to hold power." Somehow, though, they managed to retain their suspicion of Democrats, and thus continued to assume that they lacked legitimacy as office holders. Additionally, Republicans absorbed the anti-intellectualism (and often religious fundamentalism) that had previously characterized the Democrats. "If the choice was between the doctrine of evolution or the creed of creationism, Republican politicians soon learned where they had the most safety among their voters. Science was not a process that affirmed physical truths about the universe. It was an ideology that was no better and likely worse than the doctrines that seemed so identified with common sense and personal values." Among the most flagrant examples of this is Republican rejection of the finding, despite the near unanimity among climate scientists, that human activities are the prime causes of climate change.

The newly southernized Republicans thus came to reflect the least democratic, and least justifiable, features that had characterized each of the parties. They "found their worst fears confirmed regarding Democratic legitimacy with the election of Barack Obama." Some saw him "as a Socialist usurper. Others concluded that he was not even a citizen but rather a kind of Manchurian candidate out to destroy everything good in America." They had harbored similar feelings about Bill Clinton, even to the extent of harming themselves by impeaching a popular president, failing even to get a majority in the Senate to convict, when a conviction required two thirds of the Senate.

They saw Obama as representing everything they had feared, and in addition, he was black. They decided "that in the profound national crisis" brought on by his election, "the rules of American political life no longer applied." They acted accordingly, and tossed the rulebook aside. "Any means—pervasive filibusters in the Senate to block nominations, state legislation to cut back or bar minorities from the polls, changes in constitutional law to enhance the power of corporate money—should be followed to the desired end of the Republican president and a Congress with GOP majorities in both houses. That strategy went into effect once President Obama was in office." Gould remarked in 2014 that "its end is not yet in sight."[18] That, remember, was before Trump.

Gould is a compelling writer, and an excellent historian of the presidency. Even in this general survey of party history, his necessarily brief treatment of Lincoln, the first Republican to fill the office, is thoughtful and among the most perceptive of writings on the Civil War president—including many of the extensive Lincoln biographies. He asks whether the cost may have been too great to pursue the horror of the Civil War, when skeptical observers contend that slavery could perhaps have been ended in some other manner that did not involve 600,000 deaths. Perhaps in order to avoid being abrasive, he does not argue that southern leaders had become so obsessive in their determination to maintain—and in fact to extend—slavery that the chances of any such accommodation at best were miniscule, and likely nonexistent.

He nevertheless does counter the skepticism effectively, pointing out that such critics never deal with a fundamental issue. They never explain why they think "black Americans should have been asked to endure more decades of bondage and its cruelties as their contribution." Regardless of the many flaws of the Republicans, their equivocation and frequent racial prejudices, "the Republican Party was on the right side of the historical argument in the 1850s and their opponents were not." Bringing his analysis to the issues of today, he bluntly—and correctly—points out that Republicans who now turn to "neo-Confederate arguments for state rights and limited government separate themselves from the founding traditions and moral high ground of their party."[19]

Gould credits the Republicans with expanding the economic power of the national government. Lincoln signed into law the first income tax in American history, and also legislation establishing the foundation for a national system of banking and currency. He and the Republicans encouraged transcontinental transportation—the railroads—without which the country would have stagnated. To be sure, these came at the expense of the continent's native population, as did the Homestead Act providing free land for settlers, and "dispersing public land in the West." It bears repeating, that reflecting a similar concern for the people—and it should be noted, for the environment as well—Lincoln signed legislation creating the Department of Agriculture, and a Morrill Act creating land-grant universities so that higher education would be available to those outside the political and economic elites.[20]

The bad side of some of these nationalizing actions was that as time passed, Republicans became increasingly oriented toward business interests to the extent of paying less attention to the peoples' needs.[21] "Anarcho-libertarian-capitalists"—to mention one of the several names those who roundly (and absurdly) decry "statism" adopt for themselves—condemn Lincoln for building up governmental strength at the center. The Republican association with business interests bothers them much less. Those who have a more realistic and less romantic view of "state rights," recognize that if states were to have retained all their power, there could never have been an outside force to counter slavery; slavery would have continued, and very likely would still characterize the south. Moreover, without a strong national government, there would be even less ability to control multi-national corporations. The romantic view of small self-sufficient units free from an effective national government ignores the fact that unchecked corporate power, both national and multi-national, would crush such balkanized units completely.

Despite some political repression under the Lincoln administration, there was relatively little, considering the turmoil of a civil war. If ever there were an argument for suspending a national election, Lincoln could have used the crisis conditions as an excuse to do so. Fortunately for the country, he gave no serious thought to it. He showed restraint and commitment to American ideals during a time when the constitutional system, itself, was not only threatened, but actually under direct attack.

For an unsettling look into what the Republican Party has become, compare Lincoln's restraint this with a recent report from *USA Today* on August 10, 2017:

> A poll found that 52% of people who identify as or lean Republican said they would support postponing the 2020 election to ensure that only eligible citizens could vote if it was proposed by President Trump.

> The survey, conducted by two academics and published in the *Washington Post* on Thursday, interviewed a sample of 1,325 Americans from June 5–20 and focused on the 650 people who said they were or leaned toward the GOP.

The poll also found that 56% said they would support such action—which would be taken to stop alleged voter fraud—if it was supported by both Trump and Republican members of Congress (https://www.usatoday.com/story/news/politics/onpolitics/2017/08/10/52-percent-republicans-would-support-postponing-2020-election/555769001/).

One can hope that this is not accurate. It would be necessary to study the questions, the methodology, and the like, and even to repeat the study, to be sure that it is not an outlier. If this poll reflects reality, however, the Republican Party has sunk lower, and the country is in far greater danger, than even alarmists have recognized.

Gould's treatment of the Emancipation Proclamation and the Civil War Amendments is correct, but restrained. Reading it fails to convey the truly radical nature of the executive action that reached deeply into the states, and revised some of their most fundamental institutions. He does note, though, that Lincoln signed the Thirteenth Amendment outlawing slavery, "although he did not have to do so." Presidents have no official role in constitutional amendments, and the signature reflected Lincoln's deep commitment that ensured that no future president could undo the Emancipation Proclamation. Gould also recognized the importance of the Gettysburg Address that re-oriented the understandings that Americans had of themselves, and put the country on the road—however slowly, haltingly, and fitfully—toward equality and a multi-racial society.[22]

Gould is careful not to read twentieth- and twenty-first-century practices into the workings of nineteenth-century political conventions. It is the rare writer who understands this. It is common to read that Lincoln "dumped Vice President Hannibal Hamlin from the 1864 ticket," or comments to that effect—in fact, see the discussion above for an example. No evidence supports this, and it would have been uncommon for a candidate to be permitted to choose his running mate. Gould notes, correctly, that "the delegates dumped Hamlin and selected Andrew Johnson from Tennessee to run with Lincoln" (pp. 31–32). It was a disastrous choice, but the responsibility for making it was the convention's.

One observation from Gould, normally so careful, is puzzling. When Lincoln ran for re-election in 1864, he "won all but three states," but, Gould says, "he received just 55 percent of the popular vote, attesting to the residual strength of anti-Republican sentiment" (p. 32). This conclusion misrepresents Lincoln's electoral strength. By American standards, and certainly by nineteenth-century American standards, it was a landslide. Presidential elections in our relatively closely divided country never have the kind of spread that a novice might think. In only one election prior to Lincoln's 1864 victory did the winner have a greater popular-vote majority than Lincoln's. Only four presidents in U.S. history have reached 60% of the popular votes, since they began to be recorded in 1824: in reverse chronological order, they are Richard Nixon in 1972; Lyndon Johnson in 1964; Franklin Roosevelt in 1936; and Warren Harding in 1920. LBJ's 1964 victory is the only time a candidate has reached 61%.

Lincoln's 55% of the vote in 1864 was greater than any of his predecessors received, except Andrew Jackson. In 1828, Jackson's vote was barely higher (it was barely lower in 1832). No other president reached or exceeded 56% until Theodore Roosevelt did so in 1904, and of all the other presidents between Lincoln and TR, only Grant exceeded Lincoln's percentage. Thus, considering the nature of American elections, Lincoln's victory was a substantial one.

Still, Gould had a point. American political society commonly is more closely divided than it might appear, and although in terms of the history of presidential contests he was mistaken, viewed from another perspective he was correct to warn that a defeated minority more often than not remains highly competitive. "Consensus" rarely, if ever, characterizes American politics when dealing with some of its most fundamental issues.

Gould's treatment of the period from Lincoln to the end of the century is far better than that of most scholars, who repeat errors from others rather than examining the facts. Ulysses Grant is a case in point. "Much of Grant's sour reputation in the White House," Gould writes, "arose from pro-southern scholars who painted his tenure as one of unalloyed failure and weakness. More recent investigation of his eight years provides a more balanced portrait of his presidency. Grant faced a daunting set of circumstances in the South as Democratic resistance to blacks in politics hardened during the 1870s." He also inherited a situation in which his predecessor, Andrew Johnson, had effectively destroyed Reconstruction, and made it impossible for Grant to facilitate the development of a two-party system in the south. He also faced resistance from some of his own party, "Liberal Republicans," who had failed to secure jobs in his administration, and were strongly interested in civil service reform, but not at all in civil rights for citizens of African descent. Grant failed to protect black citizens adequately "from Democratic terror tactics and intimidation." Nevertheless, "there was only so much the president and the remaining Radicals in Congress could do to stem the shift of national attention away from the issues of Reconstruction."[23]

Another major corrective regarding presidential reputation comes with Gould's examination of the presidency of Benjamin Harrison. Instead of being a president who was simply subservient to Republican leaders, as Richardson indicates, he was an activist who among other things attempted "to safeguard the voting rights of black Americans in the South." He succeeded in getting a bill through the House, but ultimately failed after Republicans gained control of Congress. His first 2 years, though, were a time of substantial accomplishment. Ironically, the Democrats could say that, under Harrison, the "Republicans were the party of higher taxes and excessive government spending."[24] Harrison joined with many other Republicans to argue that "using the power of the national government to relieve the suffering of the unemployed made sense." He said that "the Republican theory has been all along that it was right to so legislate as to provide work, employment, comfort to the American workingman. We believe the National Government has a duty in this respect." His Democratic predecessor, and also successor, Grover Cleveland, took sharp exception. Harrison's "position was in marked contrast to the unwillingness of the Cleveland administration to take any direct steps to ease the effects of hard times, to put people back to work, or even to understand the plight of those unemployed."[25] This is a perfect example of the switch in positions of the two parties over the century or so that was to follow.

The rest of *The Republicans* is a thoughtful and well-presented history of the Republican Party through its course of since the 19th century. The most substantial of all Gould's insights is that Republicans, regardless of other circumstances, do not accept the validity of Democrats as office holders. This is crystal clear with regard to their treatment of both Presidents Clinton (whom they impeached) and Obama (whom they libeled as a foreigner, an anti-American, and even as the personification of evil).

Such an attitude is understandable with respect to the party's early years, because the Democrats had been the party of secession—which Republicans considered treasonous—and subsequently, for decades was the party of Jim Crow and racial discrimination. In modern times, though, any basis it retains is based on fantasies so wild as to qualify as hysteria. In fact, insofar as they affect either party today, secession, "Jim, Crow" (in the form of voter suppression), and racial discrimination are much more likely to be found among Republicans, than Democrats.

Nevertheless, Gould argues, Republicans have retained this mind set. The fact that Democrats have shed their sordid past is irrelevant, as is the fact that much of that sordid past now has been absorbed by their own Republican Party. Regardless of the lack of rationale, the firm belief that Democrats have no right to hold office has led Republicans to shed all restraints in their efforts to keep them from power.

Gould is harsh in his criticism of Republican practices, but one does not have to read Gould to recognize that Republicans freely use tactics that they would decry as inappropriate, unfair, or even treasonous were Democrats were to do the same to them. For example, Republicans seemed hardly to have reacted at all to revelations that at least six staffers in the Trump White House had used private accounts for official emails. If it is an issue at all, it is a minor one. During the campaign, however, they portrayed a decidedly minor issue—Secretary Clinton's email practices— as grounds for prosecution, at best, and execution, at worst. Lest this seem implausible, refer to the number of Trump rallies at which he encouraged the most bloodthirsty reactions, with cries of "Jail her," or even "Hang her!" Hypocrisy appears to be too mild a description of what has become routine among Trump Republicans.

The greatest shock to the GOP came with Barack Obama's election. His "nomination produced a visceral negative reaction that shaped the next several years of American politics," with currents that clearly recalled themes "of antiblack feeling, rooted in the Old South in the nineteenth century, that simply looked with horror at the prospect of a black man in the Oval Office."[26] Crowds at Republican rallies certainly had practice when they directed venom to Secretary Clinton; they had previously directed it toward President Obama. "Off with his head," they frequently screeched, obviously reflecting an overt sentiment that Obama deserved the death penalty—simply for the effrontery of being president. This was a violation of all norms of American politics. By 2016, Republican viciousness was practiced and ready for Trump as he stimulated crowds so as to thunder their abuse of Hillary Clinton.

Gould remarks that the country faces a "fundamental crisis about the future conduct of the political system," and says this became obvious when "the revolutionary aims of the Republicans became clear." He describes the manner in which at first they professed to cooperate with the planning of the Affordable Care Act. Their subterfuge succeeded in delaying action until they generated great hostility toward the act. At that point, after its passage, they sought to sabotage it.

Any piece of complex legislation requires adjustments after implementation in order for it to function properly. With the ACA, though, the Republicans not only sought repeatedly, and unsuccessfully, to repeal it, they also refused to adopt improvements, and did everything they could think of actually to make it fail. Seeking repeal is within normal practice; working to make programs fail, is not. This was unprecedented in the American political system—at least since the Civil War—which has operated through the years on the basis of cooperation to make government function as well as possible for the good of the country. "The good of the country," is a notion that, sadly, one does not encounter frequently since the Republican Party has become the party of extremism.

Despite polls showing an Obama victory, Republicans could not believe that Romney could lose in 2012. As prisoners of their own ideology, they found ways to convince themselves that there had been fraud involved. They concluded that what they needed was more intensely conservative policies, and more obstruction.[27]

In the Republicans' fevered imaginations, having been seduced into absurd beliefs by their own lurid propaganda, there was "a pretender in the White House," and he sought to destroy the republic! "There no longer existed between Republicans and Democrats a rough consensus about the purpose of the United States. The rank and file of the Republican Party believed that Barack Obama was illegitimate and evil; that the fabric of society was being torn apart by gays, blacks, Hispanics, and liberals; and that meeting these threats by any means available was the urgent duty of all true patriots."[28] With such deluded convictions, they easily turned to tactics and strategies—and this bears repeating—that they would have immediately decried as "treason!" were Democrats to employ them. See Chapter 2 for an expanded discussion of this with supportive illustrations.

An election has come and gone since Gould published this edition of *The Republicans*, and he produced a clear warning of what might come. The outcome has been far worse than his jeremiad anticipated. A Donald Trump as president of the United States did not occur spontaneously, nor did he sweep into the office because of his charisma. He was the logical conclusion of the previous four decades of America's Republican Party.

All this brings us to MacLean's *Democracy in Chains*. In contrast to the other two studies examined here, it is not a party history, but rather is a broader work of history that provides further insights into how and why the Republican Party has evolved—or degenerated—as it has done.

Democracy in Chains provides a detailed analysis of the heretofore generally unrecognized influence of an impassioned flow of extreme right wing politics. There were a number of similar sources working in concert, but McLean concentrates upon perhaps the most important one, which generated political force, under the name of "Public Choice," from within the field of economics. That strain purporting to represent a new form of economic thought, quickly became a major force in political science as well. One should note that public choice, itself, is not monolithic, and contains various strains. McLean concentrates on that which a Virginia economist, James M. Buchanan, generated: the "Virginia School."

Buchanan inspired public choice, and spent his career in Virginia giving aid and comfort to that commonwealth's fervent effort to maintain racial segregation—despite pressure from the federal government, definitive decisions from the Supreme Court, and matters of simple decency—under the Virginia oligarchs' program of "massive resistance." That all-out effort encouraged one Virginia county to go so far as to close all public schools, thus denying every one of its children any opportunity for public education, for a period of 5 years. One might legitimately conclude that the lack of any empirical economic evidence in the founding works of public choice suggests that it began as a political effort to justify both racism and class-based discrimination. It merely masqueraded as economic thought, and at base was an attack upon the very notion of democracy.

McLean is a careful historian who has delved deeply into the history of Buchanan's work, and its influence. Her introduction describes how she came to be drawn to this study. Also, it graphically reveals the racist roots that undergirded Buchanan's intellectual edifice that came to be Public Choice Theory, and his collusion with the forces of "massive resistance" that characterized Virginia's desperate efforts to thwart racial integration, and the outside attack upon its "Southern Way of Life."

Despite allegations from some critics, she does not attack Buchanan as a racist. She points out early on that there is no explicit evidence "to suggest that for a white southerner of his day, he was uniquely racist or insensitive to the concept of equal treatment. And yet, somehow," she says, "all he saw in the *Brown* decision was coercion."[29] Rather than portraying him as unusually racist for his time and place, McLean describes the facts. They make it plain that black rights were simply unimportant to him.

Buchanan was concerned with freedom, as he defined it, and directed his work to removing the limitations upon freedom of action. He was entrepreneurial, and succeeded in attracting massive funding from billionaires and foundations that operated to support libertarian causes. His conception of freedom, though, had little or nothing to do with people in general. It meant economic freedom for wealthy power holders—the protection of property, and the right of those who had wealth to use it as they saw fit. Franklin D. Roosevelt once allegedly made a comment to the effect that he was highly suspicious of those who proclaim their adherence to "freedom," when freedom as they define it would lead to restrictions upon others. Such a suspicion would be well directed toward Buchanan and his ideas.

McLean identifies Buchanan's work as part of a massive effort that recently has been very much in evidence in the Republican Party. The result has been no less than an "attempt by the billionaire-backed radical right to undo democratic governance."[30] Jane Mayer deals in depth—and superbly—with the current situation in her *Dark Money* (for a discussion of Mayer and other work on the subject, see Chapter 3, "Shining Light on Dark Politics"). McLean speaks of a "stealth bid to reverse-engineer all of America, at both the state and the national levels, back to the political economy and oligarchic governance of midcentury Virginia, minus the segregation." The intent is "to diminish the power and standing of those calling on government to protect their rights or to provide for them in one way or another." In Wisconsin in 2011, the new Republican Governor, Scott Walker, successfully "put forth legislation to strip public employees of nearly all their collective bargaining rights. In New Jersey, Republican Governor Chris Christie started attacking teachers in startlingly vitriolic terms." Across the country, "several GOP-controlled state legislatures" inflicted serious cuts in public education, "while rushing through laws to enable unregulated charter schools and provide tax subsidies for private education." Republican legislatures in "Wisconsin, North Carolina, Louisiana, Mississippi, and Iowa ... also took aim at state universities and colleges." Along with this, "came a surge of synchronized proposals to suppress voter turnout. In 2011 and 2012, legislators in forty-one states introduced more than 180 bills to restrict who could vote and how. Most of these bills seemed aimed at low-income voters, particularly minority voters, and at young people and the less mobile elderly." She notes that one investigation said, "the country hadn't seen anything like it since the end of Reconstruction." The same tendencies appeared at the national level with the strenuous campaign to defeat the Affordable Care Act, and then, when the Act became law, to sabotage it. "When the Republicans would not agree to conduct hearings to fill the Supreme Court seat left vacant after Justice Antonin Scalia died in early 2016, even the usually reticent Supreme Court Justice Clarence Thomas spoke out. 'At some point,' he told the Heritage Foundation, a conservative think tank, 'we are going to have to recognize that we are destroying our institutions.'" All these actions reflected a national campaign.[31]

To put things in perspective—and to demonstrate that it simply is not true that the parties are equally at fault, that "they all do it," or that they both are the same—consider what happened in 1973. The Democrats could then have "stolen" the presidency, as the Republicans did a Supreme Court appointment in 2017. Spiro Agnew was forced to resign the vice presidency because of corruption, vacating the office on 10 October. President Nixon, under the terms of the new 25th Amendment, had the authority to nominate a new vice president, who would take office after being confirmed by *both* houses of Congress (filling a vacancy in the vice presidency is the only time the House is involved in confirming a presidential nomination; all other confirmations involve only the Senate). President Nixon nominated Gerald Ford, the Republican leader of the House. Congressional Democrats could have refused to confirm Ford, or any other Nixon nominee, in hopes that President Nixon would be forced out of office as a result of the Watergate scandals—which, in fact, did happen on 8 August 1974. If they had refused to confirm a vice presidential nominee, the Democratic speaker of the House, Carl Albert, would have succeeded Nixon as president. Albert and the Democrats, however, decided that it would be highly improper to seize the presidency that Republicans had won through election. Thus, they confirmed Representative Gerald Ford to be vice president, enabling him to replace Nixon as President of the United States. One would be hard pressed to discover an instance in which the modern Republican Party ever put honor ahead of expedience, especially when an enormous amount of political power is at stake.

McLean's research was considerably enhanced when she discovered "an unlisted archive" that held the late Buchanan's papers on the Fairfax Campus of George Mason University. Although much of the Buchanan-led effort seems for obvious reasons to have been rather covert, the "backdoor" to the detailed process remained relatively open, only waiting discovery. Immersing herself into the actual records, she found the blueprint for much of what recently has come to fruition, and recognized that the broad outlines of what Buchanan and his funders (including the Koch Brothers, and others) have built bore a remarkable similarity, theoretically, to the scheme that John C. Calhoun advocated in the first half of the nineteenth century.

Calhoun was the most articulate defender of the system of slavery; his sole concern was government protection of property, and property, to him, meant slaves. Note that McLean does not say that Buchanan echoed Calhoun; she says, rather, that the system he advocated was consistent with Calhoun's sole concern, protection of property at all costs, and severe limitation of government otherwise.

Many of Buchanan's followers, too, have described Calhoun as "a precursor of public choice." In fact, and this should seem ominous as well as obvious, both Calhoun and Buchanan "sought ways to restrict what voters could achieve together in a democracy to what the wealthiest among them would agree to."[32] In addition to implementing policies suppressing the vote, many Republicans have sought along the same lines to foster the idea of tax "reform" that would result in "flatter, fairer, tax."

That is an oxymoron. Any informed and objective observer will recognize that the flatter the tax—that is, the less progressive it is—the easier on the wealthy and the harder on the poor it will fall. For any given rate, the effect a flat tax will have upon a given taxpayer is directly related to that taxpayer's income. A 15% tax, for example, will be extreme burdensome for someone with an income of $10,000 to pay. It will be considerably less burdensome for one making $100,000, and insignificant for one making $1,000,000. The poor person would have to live, after tax, on a pittance of $8,500, while the millionaire will be forced to make do on a mere $850,000.

Astonishingly, there are those who argue that the poor pay too little in tax. They need to have more "skin in the game," as the absurd cliché has it. In 2002, the editorial page on the *Wall Street Journal* began to assert that those too poor to pay any U.S. income tax were "lucky duckies." Apparently, no billionaire—and no *Wall Street Journal* editorialist—ever thought of a simple way to achieve that enviable tax-free status: giving all wealth away.

Buchanan had taught that government would benefit interest groups, "rent seekers," and that only the market was ideologically neutral. He and his followers denied that there was such a thing as the "public good," because each person or each interest had a differing view that would be motivated by rational self-interest. (As a personal aside, I had a heated exchange in a public meeting in Washington, D.C. over a half century ago with Gordon Tullock, Buchanan's colleague, on just that issue. He abrasively refused to concede that the "market" is as much an abstraction, and is as much influenced by government and society, as any conception of the public good.) McLean makes that point also. "The Market," she writes, is an intellectual abstraction. "In the real world, throughout history, people had created markets, and governments had shaped those markets in various ways, always benefiting some groups more than others." She pointed out bluntly what Buchanan was doing: "leveraging the prestige of economic 'science' to reject what several generations of scholarship" had exposed.[33]

A notorious feature of the "scholarship" of Buchanan's Virginia School is that it is based solely on ideology with no empirical foundation. In fact, through the years, empirical findings have continued to demonstrate that Buchanan's public choice ideas are inconsistent with the way things work in the real world. Tullock provided a prime example of how preposterous their assertions could be. He "argued that Lyndon Johnson had undertaken the War on Poverty because he probably foresaw a fairly direct exchange of political favors for votes." Even if this were true, and it manifestly was not, would it be such a bad thing to employ government to do what the people want? To pursue the "consent of the governed?" As Buchanan and his elitist theorists concluded, though, yes it would be unacceptable. But, the very assumption had nothing to do with reality. LBJ was doing anything other than pursuing votes.

As McLean points out, LBJ knew full well that in the long run anti-poverty and civil rights programs would damage his Democratic Party by alienating what had been its base, the "Solid South." Even when Tullock made the statement, LBJ's pessimistic forecasts for Democrats were well known. LBJ was adopting policies because he recognized that those policies were the right thing to do—the moral thing to do, something unrecognized by the Virginia School. Tullock "simply presented his own biases about how the world works to discredit those he opposed. It was an old saw on the American right that the people were so dull and inert that any call for government action could come only from self-interested third parties, outside agitators—whether abolitionists, 'labor bosses,' Communists, or politicians—seeking to make personal hay"[34] (p. 98).

Along with restricting democracy in a theoretical sense, Buchanan supported "law and order" policies at home, and actively colluded with the harsh dictatorship of Augusto Pinochet, in Chile. In this, he was at one with Milton Friedman and his "Chicago Boys," who were complicit in subverting Chilean democracy. The Chileans have understood for some time that they are paying the price, even after Pinochet's overthrow. Americans in general have yet to recognize that their bill, too, will come due. When it does, it will be staggering.

Many outstanding scholars applauded *Democracy in Chains* immediately upon its publication. As could have been anticipated, however, the hard-hitting book stimulated a furious flood of opposition from Buchanan's supporters and conservative commentators. Attacks from the right were to have been expected. Similar floods of protests, highly similar in their phrasing, tactics, and the like have greeted scientists who write warning of anthropogenic climate change. Similarly, those who discovered incontrovertible causal links between tobacco use and malignancies, and others who cited the availability of firearms in the United States as correlated with deaths and injuries by such weapons, faced (and continue to face) furious opposition from lavishly funded industry shills.

Various forms of right-wing "political correctness" also emerge as part of the suppression efforts. For example, remember that in 2012 (and later in 2016), two scholars known for moderation, Thomas Mann of the centrist Brookings Institution and Norman Ornstein of the conservative American Enterprise Institute, finally decided that they had to decry "false equivalency" and identify the Republican Party alone as having gone to extremes. Although they previously had appeared widely on television news shows as expert commentators, that stopped when *It's Even Worse than It Looks/Was* appeared. They found the major shows closed to them, and their invitations halted. See Chapter 2 for a full discussion.

As for McLean, in an interview that the *Chronicle of Higher Education* published on the controversy, she describes some of the attacks she faced. An especially vicious one published information on her home. The interviewer, Marc Parry, noted that Jason Brennan—a Georgetown University philosopher behaving in a decidedly unphilosophical manner (in fact, in a manner more Trumpian than thoughtful)—went to far as to say he looked "forward to seeing Duke fire her."[35] It is important to note that none of the criticism could deny McLean's key findings: Buchanan and Gordon Tullock's association with Charles Koch, and also with the Virginia power brokers whom they fed "academic" arguments to justify racial segregation and voter suppression.

Outside the circle of those who had partisan reasons for opposition, most of the reaction to MacLean's book was highly favorable. It did, though, receive a bit of criticism from the left—demonstrating that those on the left frequently may be willing in the interest of fairness to seek out inadequacies among their own ranks. Note that this is in marked contrast to the usual practice of the right, which is rarely, if ever, encumbered by any restraint imposed by fairness. The broad—and one might even say "fervent"—embrace of Donald Trump by those who previously argued that he is unfit for public office demonstrates this conclusively.

Those left of center who criticized McLean believed that the right-wing critics had made some good points. Henry Farrell and Steven Teles asserted this in an article in VOX,[36] and later—in a perhaps more cautious article—in the *Boston Review*.[37] There, however, they conceded, with difficulty seeming almost pained to do so, that "it is not entirely impossible that McLean is right."

Examination of those "points," that the critics discerned, though, demonstrates that the critics themselves may be missing the point. Andy Seal teaches economic history at the University of New Hampshire, and writes on the *U.S. Intellectual History Blog*. He provides an especially thorough refutation, identifying three essential arguments that these critics make. First, as to McLean's characterization of Buchanan, Seal says: "A few people have pointed to some passages like the one where she refers to Buchanan as an 'evil genius,'" and the like. To be sure, that is intemperate. Seal says, though, that these things sound more like "ornamental excesses," than like "structural or logical faults. So," he says, "she thinks they're jerks. That's only a problem if we believe that the whole project is organized *for the purpose of proving that Buchanan*" and his followers are jerks. That, Seal says, seems to him to be a gross misreading.

It also seems, I might add, that this appears to be a telling example of males criticizing a woman writer for being shrill. Would they have said the same about intemperate comments from a man?

The second argument pertains to Buchanan and *Brown* v. *Board of Education*. Seal says that McLean's argument is not that Buchanan "was racist so he invented public choice." Rather, "he disliked the coercive power of the state that he saw revealed in *Brown* and its enforcement, and he kept working on the problem of how to fight that power and formulated public choice."

The third argument is in response to criticism that McLean has misquoted or distorted quotations. He examines the charges in detail, and dismisses them. At the most, he says, the examples are debatable.[38] I agree.

Among the many thoughtful treatments of *Democracy in Chains*, three stand out as superb. One is one from *The Atlantic*, "The Architect of the Radical Right," by Sam Tanenhaus, formerly editor of the Sunday *New York Times* book review section;[39] another from *The Boston Review*, by Bethany Moreton, "Kochonomics: The Racist Roots of Public Choice Theory";[40] and, also from the *Boston Review*, Marshall Steinbaum's, "The Book that Explains Charlottesville."[41] Steinbaum's approach is measured, but direct. He notes that McLean "does have quite a bit to say to economists that they do not already know," and that is that "foundational elements of their field arose out of a backlash to both the New Deal and the civil rights movement." He points out that it is "vitally important to see how the heirs of the Virginia School—and their billionaire backers—still partake in a strategy of smoke and mirrors to disguise their political positioning as academic work." His critique is detailed, and is important in full. For this essay, however, it is sufficient to provide one additional quotation: "When seen in the context of its birth—as a backlash to civil rights—it is impossible not to interpret Buchanan's Public Choice theory as a politically motivated hack job." To be sure, this is not unique. Similar themes and schemes are prevalent throughout American history. Never before, however, have such lavish funding, technology, and psychological manipulation been so powerful.

Much of the criticism of McLean appears to be beside the point. It is purely academic, and has little if any relevance to the contemporary political world. One might say that reviewers approach her book with aesthetic criticism, not with an awareness of the practical consequences that she makes so clear and compelling.

As for the Republican Party of today, it is clear that the danger it presents is acute. The party has been working systematically for decades to destroy the faith of Americans in their most fundamental political, and democratic, institutions. This was made explicit in the early 1990s when Newt Gingrich sought deliberately to generate hostility from the people toward Congress as an institution. Creating resentment toward Congress as a whole was key to his successful effort to engineer a Republican takeover of the two houses; houses that for most of the preceding decades had been Democratic.

Now, their efforts to generate cynical dismissal of our essential institutions should be obvious even to the casual observer. The party, from its president on down, openly derides any journalism that does not fawn over Trump and his aides as "fake news." Striking at the very heart of the political system, Republican leaders seek to create doubt as to the integrity of America's elections—*even when Republicans win*—by fantasizing loudly about hordes of unqualified non-citizens who overwhelm the polls all across the country. Ironically, at the same time they dismiss growing evidence that there really has been Russian activity directed at influencing our elections in an effort to sow chaos. Their refusal even to consider foreign efforts to create disruption is so flagrant as to cause some observers to suspect active collusion.

It is difficult to envision—at least in the American setting—a party more destructive of democracy than one built upon the retrograde ideologies of people such as Buchanan, funded by militant libertarians, and crafted by such unrestrained "gut fighters" (to use a term that they might actually accept) as Lee Atwater, Roger Stone, Newt Gingrich, Tom DeLay, Karl Rove, Grover Norquist, and Steve Bannon. It seems not to be hyperbole to warn that we have yet to see the worst.

Notes

1   An earlier version of this essay appears in *Poverty and Public Policy* 10 (1) (March 2018).

2   Heather Cox Richardson, *To Make Men Free: A History of the Republican Party* (New York: Basic Books, 2014), xi.

3   Douglas Egerton, *The Wars of Reconstruction: The Brief, Violent History of America's Most Progressive Era* (Bloomsbury, 2014).

4   For a corrective in this regard, see my own *Maligned Presidents: The Late 19th Century* (New York: Palgrave Macmillan, 2014).

5   Richardson, x.

6   Richardson, x–xi.

7   *Ibid.*, xii.

8   *Ibid.*

9   *Ibid.*, xiii.

10 *Ibid.*, xiv.

11 Richardson, 312–313.

12 *Ibid.*, 340.

13 *Ibid.*, 340–341.

14 Lewis L. Gould, *The Republicans: A History of the Grand Old Party* (New York: Oxford University Press, 2014), 6.

15 *Ibid.*, 3.

16 *Ibid.*, 4.

17 *Ibid.*, 4.

18 *Ibid.*, 4–5.

19 *Ibid.*, 20.

20 See *ibid.*, 26–27.

21 *Ibid.*, 24.

22 *Ibid.*, 28–30.

23 Gould, 46–47.

24 *Ibid.*, 80–86.

25 *Ibid.*, 89.

26 Gould, 345–346.

27 *Ibid.*, 346–348.

28 *Ibid.*, 349–351.

29 Nancy MacLean, *Democracy in Chains: The Deep History of the Radical Right's Stealth Plan for America* (New York: Viking, 2017), xiv.

30 *Ibid.*, xv.

31 *Ibid.*, xv–xvii.

32 *Ibid.*, 1–2.

33 *Ibid.*, 97.

34 *Ibid.*, 98.

35 Marc Parry, "Nancy McLean Responds to Her Critics," *Chronicle of Higher Education*, July 19, 2017, http://www.chronicle.com/article/Nancy-MacLean-Responds-to-Her/240699.

36 Henry Farrell and Steven Teles, "Even the Intellectual Left Is Drawn to Conspiracy Theories," *Vox*, https://www.vox.com/the-big-idea/2017/7/14/15967788/democracy-shackles-james-buchanan-intellectual-history-maclean.

37 Farrell and Teles, "When Politics Drives Scholarship," *Boston Review*, August 30, 2017; http://bostonreview.net/author/henry-farrell.

38 See Seal at http://www.publicseminar.org/2017/07/the-controversy-over-democracy-in-chains/.

39 See https://www.theatlantic.com/magazine/archive/2017/07/the-architect-of-the-radical-right/528672/.

40 See http://bostonreview.net/class-inequality/bethany-moreton-kochonomics-racist-roots-public-choice-theory.

41 See http://bostonreview.net/class-inequality/marshall-steinbaum-book-explains-charlottesville.

CHAPTER 5
COULD THE NATIONAL POPULAR VOTE INTERSTATE COMPACT SAVE US FROM THE ELECTORAL COLLEGE? AN ANALYSIS AND A WORD OF CAUTION

The Electoral College—

The electoral college must have seemed a good idea to the Founders. Most of them, of course, were uncomfortable with the idea of too much democracy. In addition, some who represented slaveholding states wanted to ensure that popular sentiment could not suddenly develop a conscience, and be impelled to interfere with what the south came to call its "peculiar institution." Others were concerned, probably correctly, that if they refused to cater to slaveholders, they would never be able to design and implement a constitution at all. So, a carefully crafted Constitution with many virtues did emerge, and did place the fledgling country on a path that, despite enormous obstacles, would lead it to greatness.

The much-criticized electoral college has been in place since the Constitution, which established it. It assigns to each state a number of electoral votes equal to the number of members that state has in Congress. Since each state has two senators, and regardless of size is guaranteed to have at least one representative, the smallest number of members each state can have in Congress is three. Therefore, the smallest states each have three electoral votes.

Currently, there are seven such states: Alaska, Delaware, Montana, North Dakota, South Dakota, Vermont, and Wyoming. The other states range up to California, with 55. Under the Constitution's Twenty-Third Amendment, the District of Columbia is also assigned electors equal to the smallest state, so it, too, has three electoral votes. To win, a presidential or vice presidential candidate has to acquire a minimum of 270 electoral votes, that is, one more than half of the total number of electors, 538.

So, what the Constitution did was to saddle the fledgling country with an awkward, complicated, and undemocratic institution that would become increasingly confusing to its citizens. Worse, that electoral college would become increasingly dangerous—as the bizarre election results of 2016 demonstrated.

There have been other failures. In 1800 and 1824, the electoral college was unable to produce a winner, and in 1876, it initially failed causing Congress to step into the process. The tie that took place between Jefferson and Burr in the 1800 election led in 1804 to a correction to the Constitution: The Twelfth Amendment. A minor procedural revision brought a substantial change in the workings of the system of presidential choice. Henceforth, the Constitution required electors to cast separate votes for president and for vice president, rather than simply casting two that were undesignated. The 1800 tie threw the choice into the House of Representatives, which chose Jefferson to be president. There is little, if any, doubt that the outcome was a good one.

In 1824, there were multiple candidates, none of whom received an electoral college majority, so the House once more (and for the last time, thus far) chose the president. That choice again was a person of quality, John Quincy Adams. One of the losing candidates in 1824, Andrew Jackson—who actually had the most popular votes and the most electoral votes, although not enough to win—was furious. He argued that the electoral college should be eliminated and the popular vote should determine the winner. The issue more or less vanished when Jackson was elected overwhelmingly in 1828, and again in 1832.

As a historical note, in neither of these elections, 1800 or 1824, did the electoral college fail to choose the vice president. In 1800, when the House chose Jefferson to be president, Aaron Burr was the runner-up, and thus became vice president under the Constitution's original provision. In 1824, under the provisions of the Twelfth Amendment, electors cast separate ballots for vice president, and John C. Calhoun was the winner. The only time the electoral college has failed to select a vice president was in 1836. In that year, Martin Van Buren had sufficient electoral votes to become president, but his running mate, Richard M. Johnson, who was controversial in the south, failed to get an electoral college majority of the vice-presidential ballots. The selection then, for the first and thus far only time, fell to the Senate, as the Twelfth Amendment stipulated; the Senate selected Johnson.

The election of 1876 was arguably the most tumultuous in American history. The Democratic candidate, Samuel Tilden, won the popular vote (reflecting great suppression in the south of Republican votes in general, and those of black voters in particular). Twenty of the electoral votes were disputed: those from South Carolina, Florida, Louisiana, and a single vote from Oregon. Ultimately, in an extra-constitutional action, Congress appointed a commission of 15 members drawn from Congress and the Supreme Court to evaluate the disputed votes and settle the issue. The presumably bi-partisan commission (it turned out to have eight Republicans and seven Democrats) voted in a partisan manner on each of the 20 votes. In every instance, it voted eight to seven for the Republican, Rutherford B. Hayes, who then won by a single vote. Tilden opposed using the federal government to protect the rights of blacks, which encouraged southern "rifle clubs" to threaten a march on Washington to install him by force. President Grant, however, said that he personally would lead troops to prevent any violence, causing the southerners prudently to back down. They had no desire ever again to face Grant. The electoral verdict pleased the Republican Senate, and the Democratic House agreed to accept the outcome after assurances from supporters of Hayes that he would withdraw the remaining forces of occupation from the southern states.

The 1824 election was the first one in which there had been a significant popular vote. Initially, in most states, the state's legislature chose the electors. By 1832, however, the practice of choosing electors by popular vote was fairly well established. As democratic ideas and practices strengthened, there came to be an expectation that the electoral college and the people would make the same choice. As a rule, that has been the case. In fact, the electoral college often has given a greater margin of victory to the winner than he received in the popular vote; not always, however.

The 1888 election was an exception. Democratic President Grover Cleveland, running for re-election, narrowly won the popular vote, but his Republican opponent, Benjamin Harrison, won a substantial victory in the electoral college. There was little or no controversy, and northern states welcomed the return of the Grand Old Party (the first use of "GOP" for the Republicans).

When the Clevelands departed the executive mansion, Mrs. Cleveland said that everything should be left as it was, because they would return in 4 years. She was correct; they did. In 1892, Cleveland unseated Harrison, that time winning solidly in both the popular and the electoral votes.

Electoral College Misbehavior—

After the election of 1888, the electoral college functioned well for more than a century. There were occasional "faithless electors," who refused to cast their votes for the candidates whom they had been elected to support, but never did they affect the election's result.

Then, electoral misbehavior hit with a vengeance. In 2000, the electoral college chose the loser of the popular vote—boosted by five Republican justices on the Supreme Court who halted all recounts in a decision so partisan that that they, for the Court, limited its holding to the case under consideration; it was not, they said, to be used as a precedent. The result was the disastrous administration of George W. Bush and Richard Cheney and all that has followed from, primarily but not solely, its aggressive foreign policy in Iraq.

A mere 16 years after the 2000 fiasco, the electoral college again handed the election to the candidate who had lost the popular vote—this time by a quite substantial count of nearly three million. Worse, the losing candidate was likely the best-prepared candidate for a first term in history, and certainly one of the most able, while the winner was clearly the least experienced, and by almost any criterion one of the most unfit (if not *the* most unfit) for any high office. The clear record is that the electoral college in two of the five most recent elections went against the popular will to select, in the first instance, the most reckless, aggressive, and disruptive administration in modern history, that of George W. Bush. Most recently, it again thwarted the popular will to empower an administration that potentially could lead to such chaotic conditions as to make the Bush/Cheney years seem almost to be models of prudence.

For a short time after the debacle of 2000, there were calls to eliminate the electoral college, but for a number of reasons, such calls were muted. It was the first such failure in more than a century, the winning candidate was experienced and seemed to come from the political mainstream, liberals and Democrats tend to be more willing than their opponents to accept outcomes and hope for the best, and then the terrorist attacks on 9–11 triggered the usual American tendency to "rally around the flag" in times of crisis. To his credit, President Bush stepped into the limelight, and for the first time—and for the time being—appeared to be truly presidential. Moreover, only the most pessimistic of observers then could have anticipated the torrent of violence that would result from the Bush/Cheney foreign policy.

Things were starkly different as 2016 drew to an end. Even the harshest criticism of Bush/Cheney places that administration only into the worst-case scenario that might be anticipated for the American presidency. It was an extension and an intensification of themes that had already been present in varying degrees through the years: poor and dangerous policy, rashness, and all that could be aggregated under the worst possibilities of the "imperial presidency." Worst-case, yes, but not something completely foreign to any conception of the presidency as an institution.

The 2016 performance, on the other hand, represents a failure of the most catastrophic proportions. Despite state and local victories by the Republicans, Democrats did pick up seats in both the House and the Senate, so the electoral college was not reflecting huge popular support for Republicans. This is especially significant when one considers the vast efforts by Republican state governments across the country to suppress the votes that are most likely to be Democratic. It is worth noting here the Republicans' genius at succeeding in "bait and switch." The imprecision of vote counting in Florida in 2000 had been scandalous, leading to revelations of poor counts (which could have gone either way) across the country. In response to the need for better procedures, the Republicans blithely proceeded to change the subject, and proclaim loudly and against all relevant evidence, that "better procedures" meant legal measures to prevent fraudulent voting—which, for all practical purposes, does not exist except as a figment of their imagination. Republicans discarded the idea of improving vote counts and instead implemented new obstacles to voting. For decades, studies of voting behavior have demonstrated that, in general, the more obstacles there are to voting, the lower will be the turnout. The obstacles are most likely to inhibit voting by the poor, the less educated, the less wealthy, racial minorities, and those who have the least leisure. In other words, those who are more likely to vote Democratic. Whatever else may be said about today's Republicans, they do understand politics.

The Democratic presidential candidate in 2016 won the popular vote by a substantial majority, and lost only by tiny amounts in Pennsylvania, Michigan, and Wisconsin—states that had been anticipated to be in the Democratic column. This narrowness is not reflected in the electoral college results, which everywhere except in Maine and Nebraska are based on "winner-take-all." Thus, the typical Republican boast that "the people have spoken," and have chosen them, is mistaken. It was not "the people" who chose Trump, it was the electoral college; as for other offices, in most instances, it was gerrymander and voter suppression that spoke more loudly than "the people."

Out of the 58 presidential elections in America's history, Trump's electoral-vote percentage exceeded those of only 11 other presidents. Trump was wrong when he boasted that he received a greater electoral vote total than any president since Reagan. Even his two most immediate Democratic predecessors had totals exceeding his. Those were his hated enemies, Bill Clinton in both 1992 (370) and 1996 (379), and Barack Obama in both 2008 (365) and 2012 (332).

In the 2016 instance, the potential for enormous harm from the electoral college seems to overwhelm anything of the past. This has, finally, brought a great cry for a change in our system; a change that would provide a president selected by the popular vote. One does not have to conduct an opinion poll to recognize that Americans in general believe it only rational to eliminate the electoral college.

Prospects for Reform—

Regardless of popular opinion, though, reform by constitutional amendment is not likely to happen now, or in the future. Small states benefit considerably from their greater influence in the presidential choice because of the electoral college, and any elimination of the current system, or even a formal revision, would require a constitutional amendment. Such an amendment would require ratification of three fourths of the states. That means that the smallest 13 states *representing only 4.1% of the population*, if they were to line up together could block any constitutional amendment.

One way around this has been suggested; perhaps the only way short of an amendment that would empower the people as voters. It is a good-faith effort to ensure that the presidential winner will be the recipient of the popular vote. That proposal is the National Popular Vote Interstate Compact. It almost assuredly would be a major step forward, and it has the support of a number of states already. Also, *The New York Times* has given it strong editorial support, along with other major metropolitan newspapers.

The proposal is set forth exhaustively in a massive, but very inexpensively priced, book, *Every Vote Equal: A State-Based Plan for Electing the President by National Popular Vote*, written by John R. Koza and a number of others, mostly lawyers and academicians. The idea is for states (and the District of Columbia) to enter into a compact, promising to award their electoral votes to the winner of the popular vote, even if another candidate had carried the state. The wording of the compact is such that it would take effect when the number of states signing on is great enough to guarantee victory to the candidate winning the popular vote.

This is a worthy plan, but it contains a flaw that would have to be dealt with in some manner. That flaw has not been discussed in public, if indeed it has been recognized at all. Perhaps, the reason it has gone unrecognized is that most people interested in good government and popular control likely are devoted to fair play and the rules of the game. Thus, they are uncomfortable with naked partisanship, and are likely to dismiss as partisan any suggestion that numerous leaders of, and activists for, a political party might not be relied upon to abide by their agreements.

Nevertheless, the flaw is this: although the proposal for a National Popular Vote Interstate Compact is a good-faith effort, it would require good faith to operate, and the lack of good faith is not evenly distributed among political partisans, or parties. Rather, as a number of us have pointed out—most prominently Thomas Mann and Norm Ornstein in their powerful *It's Even Worse than It Looks/Was* (and as I have done throughout this book)—a determination to act in good faith has vanished almost entirely from many leaders of the Republican Party. A brief examination of some Republican actions in recent years should demonstrate that this is simply a recognition of reality, and is not a partisan observation.

The argument is not that all Republicans act irresponsibly or with undue partisanship, nor that Republicans are less honorable than those in other parties. It is rather that extremist elements have gained control of the party. They have caused both party leaders and legislative bodies with Republican majorities to act in defiance of understood norms, and to have chosen obstruction instead of policy improvement as a major party goal.

Republican leaders have pursued power over policy. Certainly, both parties now misuse the Senate filibuster, making it routine. The filibuster is a parliamentary device that historically—until quite recently, in fact—was a rare occurrence. Republican determination to obstruct, particularly under President Obama, made them resort to the filibuster for any Democratic proposal. The Democrats escalated their use of the technique in self-defense, so that now it has become the conventional wisdom that to pass the Senate, nearly any measure "requires 60 votes."

Another example may be seen in confirmation of presidential nominations. In 2009, Republican leader Mitch McConnell demanded of the Democrats that all their nominations be subjected to intense scrutiny. Now that nominations are coming from a Republican, McConnell considers such vetting to be unimportant, and that only Democratic "sore losers" think otherwise. Senator James Inhofe, Republican from Oklahoma, has even argued that a nomination from Trump should be enough by itself to justify confirmation.

Especially outrageous has been the Republican practice of holding necessary increases in the debt ceiling hostage to achieve their legislative goals. It may or may not be wise for a member of Congress occasionally to cast a symbolic vote against an increase in the debt ceiling in protest of a specific policy, but it is completely different to create a possibility that the debt ceiling actually might not be raised; that the United States might default on its debts. This would happen if Congress were to refuse to raise the amount that can be borrowed to pay bills already incurred. Trying to balance the budget by running up bills and then not paying them is neither practical nor ethical, but seems to be embraced by those who refuse to raise the debt ceiling, if they truly understand what the debt ceiling is.

Are these actions truly examples of bad faith? Perhaps they may simply be highly partisan, or, as in the case of the debt ceiling, overly ideological. For instances that allow of no ambiguity in interpretation, let us consider the following.

Examples of Bad Faith—

Voter Suppression. It has become notorious that Republicans have done their best to suppress the votes of populations thought likely to vote Democratic. Both parties have been guilty at times of gerrymandering to increase the effects of their parties' votes, but only the Republicans have made fervent efforts to deny qualified citizens their rights to cast their votes.

Recalling an Elected Governor. Only the Republicans have taken action to force a recently re-elected governor from office when he suddenly lost popularity as they did in October 2003 when they successfully removed California's Democratic Governor Gray Davis.

Impeachment of a President. Only Republicans have impeached a popular president for purely political, not substantive, reasons, as they did with President Clinton in a lame-duck House session in 1998. They ultimately failed to get even a majority in the Senate when conviction required support of two thirds. To their credit, some Republican senators joined Democrats in voting for acquittal.

Intransigence on Court Nominations. One of the most public demonstrations of willingness to discard the rules was the refusal of the Senate Republicans even to consider President Obama's nomination of Appeals Court Judge Merrick Garland to the Supreme Court, holding the position open for almost a year, in the hope that a Republican president could fill the vacancy. Some Republican senators even argued that if Secretary Clinton were elected, they would refuse to consider any nominee for the duration of her presidency. After the Republican candidate won, when Democrats said they would work to block any Republican extremist to the Court, Senator McConnell, who had engineered the Republican tactic to keep a seat on the Court vacant so long as President Obama remained in office, said that under a President Trump, "The American people will never permit a Court seat to remain vacant!"

Republicans assert that such overly partisan treatment of Court nominees dates back to President Reagan's 1987 nomination of Robert Bork to the Supreme Court. They have said this so consistently that it has become conventional wisdom. It is, however, mistaken. It is true that Bork was questioned roughly, and that his nomination was voted down. Bork was, however, given hearings and the opportunity to defend himself. He was not ignored, but made his zealotry clear. Republican nominations of equally zealous (although less abrasive) candidates Alito and Thomas were subsequently approved. Yes, the Thomas nomination was hard-fought, but it succeeded, and he has been on the Court now for a quarter century.

The roots of extreme partisanship regarding the Court go back at least to 1968. Chief Justice Earl Warren announced his intention to retire upon the selection of his successor. President Johnson sought to elevate Associate Justice Abe Fortas to the Chief's position, but that nomination failed for a number of reasons. Republicans then pointedly made it known to LBJ that they would block any nomination for the remainder of his presidency, and he made none.

Redistricting Mid-term to Create More Republican Seats. When Tom DeLay was majority leader in the U.S. House of Representatives, he wanted more Republicans in the chamber. Therefore, in his home state of Texas, he poured money into state legislative elections, hoping to secure Republican majorities. He succeeded. When the Texas legislature came under the control of Republicans (it historically had been Democratic, as a reflection of dynamics that had been in place at the state level since after the Civil War), he and the state Republicans imposed a "mid-census redistricting plan" on Texas's congressional districts. Redistricting traditionally comes following the decennial census. Instead of waiting for the 2010 census, even though the state recently had redistricted, the new plan was gerrymandered specifically to elect as many Republican U.S. representatives as possible. The result was that in 2004, Texas elected five more Republicans to the U.S. House than were in its previous delegation, thus solidifying Republican power.

Speaker Gingrich's New Calendar. When Newt Gingrich became speaker of the House, he changed the calendar to make it feasible for representatives to return home every weekend. He encouraged Republican members not to reside in the District of Columbia, where they would be likely to socialize with Democrats. Previously, Republicans and Democrats would fight issues on the floor, but be friendly outside the chamber. Their friendships often transcended partisanship. Gingrich argued that this was inappropriate; politics was war. It was not sufficient to win on matters of policy; rather, the goal was to destroy the enemy, and Democrats were the enemy. Cooperation for the good of the country, compromise to achieve effective policies, to a large extent became things of the past. Socializing with Democrats was unacceptable.

They were no longer to be considered mere opponents, who were equally devoted to good government. They were to be obliterated. Therein lay many of the underpinnings of the foundation upon which the intense Washington partisanship flourished. Gingrich's strategy of creating disrespect for Congress as an institution also contributed mightily to the cynicism that now exists with regard to American institutions generally; a cynicism that surely was related to the bizarre election results in 2016.

A Truly Outrageous Example of Political Perfidy. In recent years, fueled by infusing of torrents of cash from right-wing extremists, the state of North Carolina turned from a moderate swing state to one with an ultra-conservative government. Its excesses were such, that a Democratic candidate for governor fought a hard race in 2016, and after much turmoil and recounting, ultimately was declared the winner. The Republican legislature, therefore quickly passed laws greatly curtailing the governor's authority, which the outgoing, defeated, lame-duck, Republican governor immediately signed into law. The new, Democratic, governor has filed a lawsuit alleging that the legislature's actions violated the state constitution. The outcome is not yet clear. What is clear, however, is that, regardless of law or tradition, the Republicans demonstrated that they will stop at nothing to retain power.

Examples that Go Beyond Bad Faith:
Republican Actions that They Would Quickly
Call Treasonous if Taken by Democrats—

Richard Nixon's Election in 1968. It has long been known that Republican agents in 1968, through Anna Chennault, an activist with ties to conservative forces here and in the far east, convinced the government of South Vietnam to boycott the Paris peace talks to prevent a possible ending of the Vietnam War during the Johnson administration. The goal was to prolong the war, and make a presidential victory by Vice President Hubert Humphrey less likely. LBJ was aware of this, but Republican candidate Richard

Nixon expressed horror, and denied any knowledge of the plot. President Johnson, without solid proof, chose the honorable course of action, and did not make the information public. Recent revelations, however, make it clear that Nixon, himself, not only knew of the plot, but approved it. Nixon, of course, may have won, regardless, so it is not definite that the election was "stolen." It is definite, though, that he and his henchmen were willing to prolong a war, costing many lives on both sides, for reasons of partisan politics.

Ronald Reagan's Election in 1980. Similar to the initial Reagan victory, there is strong circumstantial evidence, although no "smoking gun," that Reagan's supporters dealt with Iranian officials and persuaded them to delay the release of Americans taken hostage so that the Carter administration's negotiations would not bear fruit in an "October surprise," and boost Carter's re-election chances. These allegations emerged in 1991, and suggested that Reagan's aides had promised arms to the Iranians, and that Vice President George Bush (a former director of the CIA) had participated in the arrangement. Bush strongly denied it. The fact that the Reagan administration did, indeed, supply arms to the Iranians bolstered the charges, as did the timing of the hostage release: with a final insult to President Carter, the Iranians held the hostages until the very last minute, releasing them just as his presidency ended. In October 1991, the Senate voted to conduct an investigation into these charges. The next month, however, Senate Republicans blocked the funding, so there was—and has been—no investigation.

Arms to Terrorists by the Reagan Administration. Although President Reagan proclaimed firmly to the public that he would never negotiate with "terrorists," the well-known Iran–Contra scandal late in his presidency revealed that not only did his administration deal with terrorists who kidnapped Americans and held them hostage, but as Reagan was forced to admit his administration actually supplied those kidnappers with arms that they could in turn use against Americans. Such an action would seem literally to be giving "aid and comfort" to the nation's enemies. No Democrat, however, filed a motion for impeachment, nor, of course, did anyone else.

Officials in Administration of George W. Bush Expose Undercover CIA Agent to Retaliate Against Her Husband.

Senate Republicans Send Letter to Iranian Leaders Urging them not to Negotiate with, and to Ignore, the President of the United States. In March 2015, Senator Tom Cotton addressed a letter to Iranian leaders, arrogantly lecturing them on the U.S. Constitution, urging them to come to no agreement with the Obama administration, and threatening that Obama's successor could reverse any agreement "with the stoke of a pen." The president, of course, under the Constitution, develops American foreign policy. Nevertheless, 47 Republican senators signed the unprecedented document.

The Republican Speaker of the House of Representatives— Without Informing the President or the Department of State— Invited a Foreign Head of Government to Speak to a Joint Session of Congress with the Purpose of Undercutting the Foreign Policy of the United States. In January 2015, without informing anyone and certainly without the president's approval, the speaker tendered the invitation. Numerous authorities deemed the unprecedented action to be unconstitutional. The speaker indicated that failure to inform the president was deliberate, not accidental. At the very least, it was consistent with the disrespect that Republicans recently have shown for Democratic presidents, even ignoring the executive branch when possible.

The 2016 Republican Candidate for President Openly Urged the Russians to Interfere with the Election on His Behalf to Defeat Secretary Clinton. Regardless of the extent of Russian computer hacking and meddling in an American election, it is completely clear that the Republican candidate did, indeed, invite them to do so. Even if this were a joke, which is debatable, it was worse than inappropriate.

The Republican Director of a Federal Law Enforcement Agency Directly Intervened, Twice, and Openly, in the Presidential Election. Whether deliberately or not, the FBI director violated Department of Justice policy and interfered in the election to damage the Democratic candidate's campaign. He first announced that there was no evidence that any reasonable prosecutor would use to bring charges against Secretary Clinton. Then, however, he proceeded to condemn her, giving clear indication that he wished he had been able to prosecute. Later, he announced that additional emails had been discovered, only to announce subsequently—too late for any effect on the election—that they contained nothing new. Ms. Clinton has indicated that she believes this responsible for her very narrow defeat (despite the substantial victory in the popular vote). There will never be any way to be certain. What is certain, though, is that, regardless of the FBI director's intention, whether it was malice, clumsiness, or an effort to placate conservative critics within and outside his agency, his actions not only were unprecedented, but they reflected elements of an FBI coup on behalf of the Republicans.

The Fatal Flaw that Must be Remedied if the National Popular Vote Interstate Compact Is to Achieve Its Goal of Empowering the People, as opposed to the Explicitly Undemocratic Electoral College—

The Compact would require states that sign on to agree to award their electoral votes to the winner of the popular vote, regardless of the vote in the state, itself. States that sign on to the Compact agree to do so.

In order to assess the feasibility of the proposal, and whether it would work as intended, the willingness of some political actors to do whatever would secure their power must be taken into consideration. This is not a partisan statement, although there is certainly an imbalance in the willingness of political parties to misbehave. As Lewis Gould, the acclaimed historian of the Republican Party put it in his most recent study, *The Republicans: A History of the Grand Old Party*, put it in 2014 (and remember, this was before Donald Trump burst on the political scene as the equivalent of a volcano, a hurricane, an enormous asteroid strike, or perhaps a combination of them all): people "have failed to notice that one major party has decided that democratic procedures should no longer constrain its behavior. Thus a major breakdown in how American politics works has gone unremarked."

Thus, regardless of the state's popular vote, any compact, or any previously agreed arrangement to honor the national popular vote the legislature of a state retains the power to do whatever it chooses to do with regard to the electoral votes of its own state.

The state legislatures have the power to do this. As the Court said in Bush v. Gore:

> The individual citizen has no federal constitutional right to vote for electors for the president of the United States unless and until the state legislature chooses a statewide election as the means to implement its power to appoint members of the Electoral College.

> Moreover, continued the Court, "the state legislature's power to select the manner for appointing electors is plenary; it may, if it so chooses, select the electors itself." Once having chosen a method for selecting electors, "the state, of course, after granting the franchise in the special context of Article II, can take back the power to appoint electors."

Could anyone be confident that, given the party's recent history, a Republican legislature would abide by its word, and submit a slate of Democratic electors if the state's voters had given the majority to the Republican candidate? People who have not examined the evidence might respond that, of course, they would abide by their word. That is the American way. Examining the evidence, though, makes it clear that whether or not it is the American way, so far as the modern party is concerned, it is not the Republican way.

At this point, it might not be the Democratic way, either. Whether Democrats would remain true to their word, or whether they would point to Republicans and say that Democrats cannot afford to be bound by promises when their opponents are not, given the current ugliness of American politics could either party be trusted to set aside its interests for the public good?

Let us once again look at what evidence there is.

In fact, there is additional evidence that leaves no doubt that "good faith" is utterly powerless to restrain Republicans if it interferes with their efforts to secure power. The Court, as quoted above, makes it plain that a state's legislature has the power to select the electors it wishes, regardless of any factor. It can overrule the voters. It can go against the state's own constitution. It can change its collective mind. It could without doubt violate any compact to which it previously agreed.

In 2000, in fact, the legislature of the State of Florida planned to do just that, if a recount determined that Vice President Gore had won the state. As I have written elsewhere: Republicans in the legislature planned to choose Bush/Cheney electors, regardless of the result of any recount. USA Today reported as much on December 12, 2002. It did not come to pass because of the Court's decision the next day that made it unnecessary.

Thus, the Compact must provide explicit, severe, and self-enforcing penalties for any legislator who, in the course of an election, would violate the state's pledge to choose a slate of electors who would cast their votes for the popular-vote winner. One example might be such a penalty built into state law, providing that any legislator who did not act in good faith in this regard would immediately surrender his or her legislative seat, and be forever ineligible for elective office.

One can only hope that this does not sound either partisan or overly pessimistic. I do think the compact could work, but only if adequate safeguards are built into the framework from the start—and building such a framework would require all sides to recognize that regardless of any agreement, some form of coercion would have to be employed to force compliance with promises.

www.ingramcontent.com/pod-product-compliance
Lightning Source LLC
Chambersburg PA
CBHW070805280326
41934CB00012B/3073